Locked

Locked:
A Full-Length Play in Two Acts

by Philip Zwerling and Lorenzo Pace

LITERARY PRESS
LAMAR UNIVERSITY

ISBN: 978-1-942956-86-0
LOC: 2021930176

Cover Photo: Ron Cogswell

Lamar University Literary Press
Beaumont, TX

This play is dedicated to our ancestors and all the unnamed, unkown playwrights who never got their work published as well as the actors who were never acknowledged on stage. And to the interconnected families (Pace, Clark, Williams, Wynn, Hubbard, Thomas, Ogletree, Berry, Ellison, Zwerling, and Stoiber). We are all one human family, and Black lives matter.

A photograph of the Pace family, Dorthy Turk Pace, 1943
High resolution photography: David Kennedy Cutler

Recent Books by Lamar University Literary Press

Lisa Adams, *Xuai*
Walter Bargen, *My Other Mother's Red Mercedes*
Roberto Bonazzi, *Awakened by Surprise*
David Bowles, *Borderlore*
Jerry Bradley, *Collapsing into Possibility*
Mark Busby, *Through Our Times*
Catalina Castillion and Andy Coughlan, *Rottens, Chatterboxes, and Mayors*
Julie Chappell, *Mad Habits of a Life*
Stan Crawford, *Resisting Gravity*
Glover Davis, *My Cap of Darkness*
William Virgil Davis, *The Bones Poems*
Jeffrey DeLotto, *Voices Writ in Sand*
Chris Ellery, *Elder Tree*
Dede Fox, *On Wings of Silence*
Alan Gann, *That's Entertainment*
Larry Griffin, *Cedar Plums*
Britt Harroway, *Early Man*
Michelle Hartman, *Irony and Irrelevance*
Katherine Hoerth, *Goddess Wears Cowboy Boots*
Michael Jennings, *Crossings: A Record of Travel*
Gretchen Johnson, *A Trip Through Downer, Minnesota*
Betsy Joseph, *Only So Many Autumns*
Ulf Kirchdorfer, *Chewing Green Leaves*
Jim McGarrah, *A Balancing Act*
J. Pittman McGehee, *Nod of Knowing*
Tom Mack and Andrew Geyer, *A Shared Voice*
Laurence Musgrove, *Bluebonnet Sutras*
Benjamin Myers, *Black Sunday*
Janice Northerns, *Some Electric Hum*
Godspower Oboido, *Wandering Feet on Pebbled Shores*
Carol Coffee Reposa, *Underground Musicians*
Jan Seale, *The Parkinson Poems*
Steven Schroeder, *the moon, not the finger, pointing*
Glen Sorestad, *Hazards of Eden*
Vincent Spina, *The Sumptuous Hills of Gulfport*
W.K. Stratton, *Betrayal Creek*
Wally Swist, *Invocation*
Ken Waldman, *Sports Page*
Loretta Diane Walker, *Ode to My Mother's Voice*
Dan Williams, *Past Purgatory, a Distant Paradise*
Jonas Zdanys, *The Angled Road*

For information on these and other Lamar University Literary
Press books go to www.Lamar.edu/literarypress

CONTENTS

Introduction

We based this play on a true story. Unfortunately, we would say, because it is the unfortunate story of slavery in America and all the sadness, violence, greed, and murder that accompanied it. That story often feels like old news, distanced by a hundred years of history, even out of date today. The slaves, the slaveholders, and the abolitionists, the plantation system, the great war between the states, reconstruction, the Ku Klux Klan, and legal segregation are dead and gone, swept away by history and a newly enlightened sensibility of racial harmony reaching a climax in the 2008–2016 administration of President Barack Obama, and a post racial age. Or so some people thought. For too many people "The past isn't dead," as novelist William Faulkner wrote, "it's not even past."

The election of President Donald Trump, the rise of the Alt Right, the mayhem and murder at Charlottesville, Virginia in 2017 in a drive to 'Unite the Right', and police and vigilante shootings of unarmed Black men (104 killed in 2015 alone), give that hopeful and rosy picture the lie.

Polls, Op Ed pieces, news reports, blogs, editorials, political speeches, and TV commentaries attempt to make sense of our still 'DisUnited States of America' divided by racial hatred. None of this is news. What is news is the systemic nature of racial animosity in America: from the police enforcement of state violence in the streets to the end product of filling our prisons with Black men, stockpiled out of sight; to the genteel violence of the boardrooms that deny loans and mortgages to Black families, that redline neighborhoods and deny equal access to quality healthcare, as the COVID-19 pandemic has starkly highlighted in the disproportionate suffering of communities of color across our country.

So, we wrote a play to dramatize our fears and hopes, our reality and our ideals. A pretty weak response, no doubt, to a continuing genocide. A slender reed to build a better future. How to envision and stage 400 years of racial history since English settlers first forced African slaves ashore at Jamestown, Virginia in August 1619, slavery concurrent with the very founding of America? For America's founding, growing wealth and power was impossible without slavery. After all, who couldn't make a success of it with unpaid Black labor toiling in the fields piling up treasure in the storehouses of White owners? The richest men in America owed their wealth to the trade in slaves. Slaves became our early nation's most valuable commodity, picking the cotton to supply and clothe the world.

How many Africans did Europeans kidnap, force aboard ships, and deliver to auction blocks in the colonies? Twelve million? Twenty million ripped from their families? How many more never made it to our shores, dying in the Middle Passage of transport chained below decks? And when the the British ended the slave trade how many Black men and women did the border colonies like Virginia breed like cattle and then rip families apart to sell their children 'down the river' to deep south plantations? Black people had no rights that a White owner need respect. They could be whipped, starved, overworked, and sold. They had no rights to marry, to learn to read or write, or to worship. They stood on auction blocks like chattel and household goods, sold to the highest bidder. How do you dramatize that? If anti-Black racism lies buried deep in the souls of White people throughout the 400 year history of America (colony and country) how do you excavate and remove the stain? How do you unlock its grip and free White people of racism and Black people of their oppression?

In 2007 the University of Texas Pan American hired Phil Zwerling and Lorenzo Pace to teach Creative Writing and Art, respectively. Pace specialized in visual art (painting, collage, and sculpture) while Zwerling specialized in playwriting. Both came to Texas from previous positions in the east and each first heard the other's name at a large gathering of the College of Liberal Arts meeting in the University Ballroom to introduce some fifty new professors to their colleagues. Each department chair made a few remarks that day and pointed out their new hires. The Chair of the Art Department ran down the list of new hires and pointed out arriving colleagues. He and Pace were long time friends. He announced: "And Dr. Pace is the Black man standing against the wall over there." An audible buzz of shock and disapproval swept the room. Had he said "Black?" Can you say that word publicly?

The crowd's discomfort surprised Zwerling. After all Pace did stand out as the only Black man in the room of 200 or so mostly Latino and Anglo men and women. Calling him the Black man in the room seemed an appropriate signifier and yet it made people terribly uncomfortable.

When the two men ran into each other on campus sometime later, they fell into conversation about their work and interests. They had little in common at first glance. Pace, never without a garishly colorful shirt, a rakishly placed chapeau and jewelry around his neck wore it all with a gleaming broad smile, and a ready handshake, a buoyant soul among a grey multitude.

Zwerling worked at dressing and acting the part of the Assistant Professor whose tenure track career meant six years of probation and depended upon his colleagues' judgment and acceptance. He had no desire to stand out. But we both appreciated art, we both liked to talk about our creative work, and Pace had an eye out for a collaborator. Even a White one. You see, the theory and practice of collaboration looms large for Pace who believes collaboration is basic to the survival of our human family and without which we are doomed to division and extinction. He practices old style community organizing wherever he goes whether it be in 'pop up' audience participation musicals or African circle drumming. Zwerling usually likes to work alone when he writes. How would they ever get along?

But why shouldn't a Jew and a Christian, a White man and a Black man write a play together? Their very collaboration might serve as a model for others. Pace had a dramatic story to tell, one he had told earlier in his children's book "Jalani and the Lock" but for which he now sought a live stage. Once upon a time, slavers had kidnapped his great-grandfather, bound him in chains, transported him to America and sold him into slavery. This is the story we struggled to put on stage.

Pace's family story contained one fascinating and theatrical twist: he had in his possession, passed down through generations, the old iron lock that a hundred years before had bound the chains of his enslaved ancestor. That object excited Zwerling's imagination. In his playwriting classes he required students to create characters and then to write monologues for them. To get them started he randomly assigned their characters a vocation (i.e. 'Winter Texan,' 'police officer,' 'dog walker,' 'magician') and a physical object (i.e. a length of pipe, a fine painting, a rabbit, a head of lettuce), instructing them to use the object not as a mere prop but rather as a tool to reveal their character's inner life. Having an object literally and figuratively anchors a character onstage, gives them something to do physically while it also focuses and holds the attention of an audience. In this case the lock came loaded with freight—an audience could not ignore asking themselves to imagine the individual who writhed in its chains years ago. The lock also served symbolically as a metaphor for both the history of slavery and for the chains of contemporary racism which still bind the Pace family. The lock explained why this story should live on stage, rather than in a short story, novel, poem, or essay. The lock demanded to be seen not just described. An audience needed to measure with their own eyes the iron solidity and finality of enslavement.

Some things you decide quickly and regret at your leisure. The script went through 12 rewrites over two years. Every table reading brought new, sometimes contradictory, critiques. Did the play shoehorn too much history into 90 minutes? Whose story was it? Who was the protagonist: Mary Alice, Lorenzo, Jalani? Could it be Eva? Did people find Mary Alice too angry, too anti-White, to like? How could she not be angry at the world and everyone in it after what she had lived through? Who, or what, served as the antagonist, the obstacle to her role as protagonist? Every critic had an opinion. Some gave us real insights but at some point we had to tell them to go write their own damn play.

We wrote and rewrote. We met at the local IHOP, at Cafe 101, in various nooks and crannies of the campus thrashing out plot and arguing about details. Collaboration comes with an emotional and intellectual price. We celebrated each other's new ideas and withdrew to lick our wounds when we disagreed. We fought, reconciled and fought again. We compromised. Most importantly we agitated each other and spurred each other's imaginations. It paid off. And we've remained friends for many years.

We settled on the Inciting Incident. The death of Rev. Eddie T. Pace prior to the beginning of the play changes the world of the characters, brings them together again in Birmingham for the funeral and the reading of the will, just as, for example, the death of Hamlet the King rocks the world of Elsinore before that eponymous play begins. We chose as our Point of Attack the discovery of 'the box' by Jalani in his grandfather's desk. This mysterious box, which Daisy May tells us Eddie and Mary Alice had once so loudly argued about, sets the action of the play in motion and drives it to the climax just as King Hamlet's ghost demanding revenge leads finally to all the dead bodies (Laertes, Gertrude, Claudius, and Hamlet, Jr.) who litter the stage at the end of that play. Our climax would be the opening of the lock, the unlocking of secrets, of hate and racism, and, finally, the unlocking of love. The lock reopens by chance, after falling and striking the floor in Act 2, Scene 5. Or, is this from outside intervention, whether from God or Afenyi, or history itself...?

Our cast of characters grew as we revised. Clearly to represent a society locked in racism we needed to show its many aspects: young and old, male and female, White and Black. The writers are not their characters and yet the characters come from the writers; from some aspect of their own experiences and emotional life. As White and Black writers we created White and Black characters. As a Christian and a Jew we created Christian and Jewish characters. As male writers we created male characters and stretched to create female characters.

Mary Alice Pace, under the strain of sudden bereavement, under pressure from her son to move away from her home of many years and happy memories, plagued by nightmares of a racist history that recalls her own personal violent past, is our protagonist. She needs to free herself from the past to be happy in the present. The obstacles to her happiness are Lorenzo, Jalani, Eva, White racism ... and herself. Her need plus the obstacles she faces to fulfill her need produce conflict, the very heart of drama. In playwriting classes Zwerling asks his students to imagine their protagonist and antagonist as two scorpions trapped in a bottle—where one will win and one will die.

We wrote Lorenzo, our coauthor, into the play as a character, a dutiful but beleaguered son, a caring but domineering father and lonely widower. Jalani, the name of Lorenzo's son in real life, comes from a new generation untethered to the past, seeking his own personal fulfillment and trying to escape parental controls and family expectations. Eva, a young Jewish woman from New York, in love with Jalani, but without experience in the South, sees no color barrier to their relationship. Zwerling has written a number of plays with young female protagonists. Perhaps he wanted to see some of himself in Eva. What of Daisy May and Maisy Day? They simultaneously provide comedic relief, a love interest for Lorenzo and, in their varying shades of Blackness, signify the historical reality of White violence and rape visited upon the descendants of the slave victims. They embody also the racial standards within the Black community where some have learned to value light skinned Blacks with straight hair, thin lips, and small noses as better, prettier, more respectable, just as White people do. As the saying goes: 'If you're white, you're alright, if you're brown, stick around, if you're yellow you're mellow but if you're black, get back.'

Each of our characters is locked in their own way: Mary Alice in her haunting dreams and past rape, Lorenzo in his role as *pater familias*, the oldest male family member stuck in the uncomfortable role of autocratic son and domineering father, Jalani locked into family expectations, Eva locked into her own White privilege and Daisy and Maisy trapped first by a dependent ailing father and then by expectations of southern spinsterhood.

We gave each character a journey, an arc of development, in the course of the play. We know that the most interesting moments in our own lives come when we make a change in behavior or thought. That change may derive from our own conscious decision or be imposed upon us by others or by forces outside our control. In *Locked* Mary Alice confronts the racist violence visited upon her and her ancestors and decides to move on even accepting that others can make their own decisions: Jalani as to where he

13

goes to school, Lorenzo as to whom he will love, Eva as to how she will choose her relationships for herself. This represents no capitulation to outside forces, as Mary Alice demands to remain self sufficient in her own home. Lorenzo, recognizing his own unhappiness at Morehouse and the burden of the Pace name lets go of control, allowing Mary Alice and Jalani to make their own choices. Eva, at first trying to quietly fit in, makes the choice to stand up to the formidable Mary Alice regardless of the price she may pay. Jalani rebels against his father's dictates and nearly takes physical punishment for his resistance. Daisy May takes a leap into the unknown, possibly willing to leave behind twin and home for a new love. At the beginning of the play all the characters are locked into social expectations and family obligations. At the end each begins to walk a freedom path.

We chose our setting with some care. Sadly, we had many settings to choose from. We knew Black slaves helped build the US Capitol and the White House. It made Zwerling think of the Israelites in bondage in Egypt helping to build the pyramids. Pace had already designed a towering black granite memorial for unknown Black slaves interred in a previously unmarked mass grave unearthed recently in the heart of Manhattan. Slavery had reached into every geographical corner of the young United States, and not just the Deep South. Even our new home state of Texas had risen to power and wealth on the back of slave labor. At the outbreak of the Civil War one third the population of the state of Texas consisted of slaves forced to work without pay and under the threat of the lash on cotton plantations and ranches. While our own Deep South Rio Grande Valley had no slave history, the reason has nothing to do with any local anti-slavery sensitivity. It turns out Mexican and Mexican American labor was so cheap there that slaves did not seem necessary to the economy. But the Rio Grande River and Mexico's anti-slavery laws which began on the river's southern bank had drawn Black people to the area, following the southern route of the Underground Railroad to freedom in Mexico. Some 3,000 slaves are known to have followed that path to freedom. The Texas Rangers, celebrated in Western lore, cinema and T.V serials began as slave catchers to stop this freedom flight. In fact, the Yankees and the Confederates fought the very last battle of the Civil War not far from our Texas campus at Palmetto Ranch. The Rebs won the battle and lost the war.

In the end, we chose to go back to coauthor Lorenzo's home city of Birmingham and mined its history including the bombing of the 16th Street Baptist Church and the murder of four little Black girls on a Sunday morning, one of the most shocking crimes of the Civil Rights era. Earning the name 'Bombingham,' the Ku Klux Klan and other White supremacists terrorized this Deep South City with some 50 bombings between 1947 and 1965, usually aimed at Black people trying to integrate previously White neighborhoods. One neighborhood was targeted so often in this segregated city by these domestic terrorists that it earned the sobriquet 'Dynamite Hill." Describing the crime and the times in broad generalities must never overlook the sacrifice of four little Black girls: Addie May Collins, Denise McNair, Carole Robertson, and Cynthia Wesley, aged 11 to 14, who unwillingly gave their lives for the cause of freedom. May their names never be forgotten. There have been so many martyrs in this struggle.

As we wrote we kept aiming to raise the stakes in the play. We condensed the action to just two days so Mary Alice had to decide to stay or leave Birmingham, Jalani had to decide whether to enroll in Morehouse or NYU, Lorenzo, after years of widowhood, had to decide whether to go on a date or, as usual, stay home. Each choice, made under internal or external pressure constituted a turn in a character's life, opening and closing possibilities. We put pressure on the family to see who would crack: would Mary Alice give up her home, would Jalani give up Eva, would Lorenzo give Jalani the freedom to make his own choices or impose his will as his father had imposed his, would Eva stand up to Mary Alice to remain with Jalani, could Mary Alice overcome both her nightmares and her own trauma?

And then we complicated the action. Every writer wants to get from point A, the beginning, to point B, the end. And they too often think the best route is a straight line. We thought, yes, you have to know the beginning, Jalani discovers the box in his grandfather's desk, and we knew the ending had to involve opening the lock for all of its attendant symbolism of freedom. But which route to take to get there? We could have made it easy. Jalani and Eva could have opened the lock themselves. Or maybe Daisy May with her handywoman skills could have done it. Yet we kept asking ourselves how can we complicate this plot? How can we make the characters work harder to get from Point A to Point B to make things more interesting? First, Mary Alice denies the lock's existence and significance. Then Jalani can't open it. He throws it to Eva. Eva can't open it. Mary Alice tries to ignore its presence in the box at the reading of the will. Lorenzo digs a bit deeper. This little piece of hardware frustrates each and every character on stage. And with each failure the symbolic weight of the lock grows.

So we added subplots to the main plot of Mary Alice's racial nightmares: like Lorenzo's wish to move Mary Alice north, Jalani's fight for his personal choice of college, Eva's fight to be with Jalani, Daisy May's fight to be with Lorenzo. At a family gathering in a time of bereavement each character has something on the line, something to fight for and something, or someone, to fight against.

We developed subtext, knowing that the real meaning lies below the words that people speak. Depending upon the character, their needs, their disposition, a line of innocuous dialogue like "How are you today?" can really mean anything from "I love you" to "I hope you die" depending upon intonation and body language. The glory of theater is its collaborative nature. While a poet or fiction writer might sit alone before their computer and write, then submit the manuscript, only to see it in print in a book or magazine months later; they can only imagine a reader's reaction. As writers we collaborated with each other, tossed ideas around, imagined other plots and added and subtracted characters; we knew we would need to rely on many other collaborators—a stage director, actors, set designers, light and sound designers to flesh out their blueprint. And we would get to see our words on stage in the company of a live audience reacting in the moment to what we had written. The actors deliver much of the subtext—with their facial expressions, body language, verbal intonations—their own character interpretations based on the script but also on their own life experiences.

As we wrote the play we discovered the tangled nature of the themes we unearthed. Certainly we wanted to write about slavery, and contemporary racism and today's racial divide. But we also kept hitting up against the issue of identity and names. Deeply committed to the Pace name and all it stands for in Birmingham, Mary Alice feels ashamed of the slave names 'Ezekiel' and 'Alice' bestowed on her ancestors by their masters. They lost their own African names, as well as their language and family kinships when kidnapped and enslaved. Lorenzo sports a typically Italian name that appears untypical for an African American man. He has given his son an African name, Jalani, to remind him of his proud heritage, even though Jalani has never visited Africa. Maisy Day and Daisy May have to live with matching, rhyming names given them by parents celebrating their twin birth and confusing folks they meet. Eva rejects her last name because immigration officers at Ellis Island stripped her grandfather of his foreign sounding family name Barnovsky and gave him the more 'American' sounding name of Barnes.

Think about how each of us builds an identity. We inherit a last name from family, receive a first name from parents, grow up within an ethnic, racial, or religious group, and set roots down in a geographic place we call home. With those given circumstances we then grow our individuality, through our particular experiences, choices, and decisions. The philosopher Jean Paul Sartre wrote that 'existence precedes essence,' meaning that first we exist and then we define who we are. But we get tagged with a name, a skin color, a gender immediately and grow into that reality. What happens when that foundation of identity does not exist or gets swept away? Zwerling learned something about this firsthand while writing *Locked*. Joining the crowd he sent 23andme a mouth swab bearing his DNA and discovered that his father was not his father, his cousins were not his cousins and, even more shockingly that he had at least 15 half brothers and sisters he had never met—they had all been 'fathered' by a sperm donor, now deceased.

What do you do with that information? Your parents, also now deceased, never mentioned this little detail. They always insisted you tell the truth. Why didn't they? If they hid this from you what else did you believe that was not true? Did this explain the strains between father and son, which had seemed normal enough, that now loomed as the jealous enmity of a man who could not be a biological father? Who knows? But that's just it, you can't know. The foundation crumbles and you question both your existence and your essence. Slave or free, immigrant or native born, you do not obscure someone's ancestry without shaking the ground they have built a life on and forcing them to question their very identity and place in life. An actor once said 'how wonderful it would be to play Hamlet the night after your father has died.' How emotional as well to write about lost names days after you have lost your own. Pace did his own DNA research which revealed this African American had British, Spanish, and Portuguese ancestors.

We raised up so many issues: racism, parental authority, love, old and young, but our spine, the theme that holds the play together is freedom.

Surely this is the theme of African American history: the march from slavery through segregation, police brutality, social disenfranchisement, economic oppression to a promised land of freedom and equality. Each of the main characters struggles for their own freedom and finds it: Mary Alice relieved of the past, Lorenzo absolved from responsibility for his mother and child, Jalani free of a college he had not chosen, Daisy May free from her spinsterhood, and Eva free to be with the man she loves. Their individual stories stand for the aggregate mass of people, White and Black, struggling to free themselves from social, political, and economic serfdom.

The play's resolution imagines a future of freedom writ large and small, societal and individual. Each character has trod a path of disappointment and frustration and has freed themselves for a new day.

When we had finally written draft 12 and discovered what we wanted to share with an audience we stumbled over unexpected impediments. Where would we find actors? Most university theater programs, even today, present a monochromatic pale color. Few such programs, outside of historically Black colleges, which comprise less than 2% of all U.S. colleges, can boast of Black theater students. Segregated not by law but by ... what? Majority White theater programs remain a legacy of unexamined racism.

Now, in deep south Texas we did have a 95% Mexican American population in the community at large and an 85% Mexican American student body on campus, in a county, Hidalgo, where 38% of people live below the poverty line. That reality and history demand another play.

We refused to have White actors read for Black parts. The University had several years before put a Latino actor onstage in blackening makeup to stage *To Kill A Mockingbird*. We didn't want to go that route.

In that case, we acted as our own casting directors. When posters and announcements didn't bring in actors, we went out for lunch time forays around campus waylaying anyone who looked Black and telling them what a great part we had for them. We replayed our recruitment efforts at local grocery stores, doctors' offices, and street corners. Have you ever approached a stranger asking "Are you Black and do you like to act?" We can assure you, you lose your normal inhibitions quite quickly.

Pace hit the several historically Black churches in the Rio Grande Valley at Sunday services to talk about our project and recruit interested folk. Truth be told, we met an awful lot of interesting people, many of them outside our usual experience as academics. Finally we had a cast. But a cast of what? They weren't actors: they were school teachers, students, choir directors, a car dealer. None of them had ever been on stage before. Our director, theater instructor Peter 'Trey' Mikolasky, had warned us that not just anyone could act. In time, we discovered the truth of this for ourselves. So we settled for a Readers' Theater Production with the cast on stage behind individual podiums and a large audience in attendance. We saw that the play worked and the characters came alive and the story captured the audience.

This is our play. We hope it affects you as much as it did us in creating it.

Philip Zwerling   Lorenzo Pace

For more insight we recommend two books, one by a Black author and one by a White author, naturally:

Before the Mayflower by Lerone Bennett, Jr. and
The Lost Cities of Africa by Basil Davidson

LOCKED

A Full Length Play in Two Acts
by Philip Zwerling and Lorenzo Pace

Locked was first presented as a Reader's Theater Production at the University of Texas Pan American Albert Jeffers Theater on October 23, 2014. The cast was as follows:

Mary Alice Pace	Loretha Laws
Lorenzo Pace	Tomeker D. Robertson
Jalani Pace	Demetrius Davis
Eva Barnes	Victoria Peña
Daisy May Benson	Hope Hernandez
Maisy Day Bensen	Tamara Bryant

The play was directed by Peter "Trey" Mikolasky
Lights designed by Giovanni Salinas
Poster Art by Libni Cortes
Stage Manager, Cyanne Trevino
Assistant Stage Managers, Justin Gonzalez and Carter B. Copeland

Characters and Setting

Characters:

Mary Alice Pace	75 years old, lives in Birmingham, Alabama
Lorenzo Pace	her son, 49 years old, lives in New York City
Jalani Pace	his son, 17 years old, lives in New York City
Eva Barnes	Jalani's White girlfriend, 17, lives in New York City.
Alice Pace	great-grandmother to Lorenzo, same actor as Mary Alice
Afenyi	former slave, same actor as Mary Alice
Daisy May Bensen	37 year old neighbor to May Alice and twin to Maisy Day, but she looks White
Maisy Day Bensen	37 year old neighbor to May Alice and twin to Daisy May, but she looks Black

Slave catcher/slave auctioneer/Thomas Hardaway/funeral director
all played by same White actor

Mary Alice Hardaway same actress as Eva

Two soldiers

Actors as animals

Gospel choir

African Dancers

Setting:

Birmingham, Alabama parlor of Bishop Eddie T. Pace and West Africa

Time: 1991 in Birmingham, Alabama and 1847 in West Africa

Pre-show music: Gospel Choir sings (live or recorded).
Songs like "We Shall Be Changed," "We Shall Overcome," "We Shall not Be Moved" might be used.

Act 1

Scene 1

SETTING: A Sunday morning in Birmingham, Alabama, September 15, 1963.

OFF STAGE: Suddenly a loud explosion. Sounds of broken glass, people running, screams, people crying. Fire engine sirens.

AT RISE: Out of the smoke and noise emerges AFENYI, wearing colorful cloth and carrying a basket. SHE wears a very unique necklace we will see each time SHE appears. SHE looks bewildered, lost. SHE sets down her basket. SHE enters the smoke and after a long beat reemerges with a girl's dress shoe stained with blood. SHE inspects it. SHE picks up HER basket. SHE looks again at the shoe in HER hand and extends HER arm to the audience as if offering them the shoe. SHE looks back into the smoke as if to see the devastation. AFENYI shakes HER head sadly and slowly exits.

Joan Baez singing "Birmingham Sunday" is heard.

Simultaneous with this song, projections on stage from September 15, 1963, photos of the demolished church, photos of the four dead girls, photos of people grieving, newspaper headlines, Ku Klux Klan marching, Governor George Wallace standing in the schoolhouse door against integration, Martin Luther King and his "Letter from a Birmingham Jail." Then the song "Sometimes I feel Like a Motherless Child."

Act 1

Scene 2

SETTING: A summer afternoon in the Birmingham, Alabama parlor of the recently deceased Bishop Eddie T. Pace in 1991. The room is dark but lived in and welcoming, perhaps 30 or more years behind the times. There are chairs, a sofa, a large roll top desk, heavy drapes or blinds and thick rugs on the floor, some bookcases and a fireplace. Three pictures are prominently displayed on one wall: Jesus, President John F. Kennedy and Martin Luther King. Several colorful homemade quilts are draped on the sofa and chair.

AT RISE: a doorbell is heard ringing off stage. MARY ALICE crosses parlor.

MARY ALICE

I'll get it.

(Door is heard opening)

Come in, come in. You look sooooo lovely, Maisy. So pretty. (then grudgingly) And you too Daisy.

(door is heard closing)

(stage whisper) Yes, he's here. You're just in time.

(MARY ALICE reenters the parlor followed by DAISY MAY and MAISY DAY, shouting into house)

What a surprise! Guess who's here, Lorenzo? We have visitors! (to the BENSEN SISTERS) Sit down, sit down, girls. Make yourselves at home. (shouting) Lorenzo!

LORENZO

(shouting from off stage) Coming Mama.

(Lorenzo enters, sees the sisters to his surprise)

Oh ... Hello.

MARY ALICE

Lorenzo, you remember my very good neighbor friend Maisy Day

LORENZO

Of course, how wonderful to see you again.

MARY ALICE

—and her sister, Daisy May.

LORENZO

Yes, Mama.

(greeting each formally in turn with a hand shake and a quick hug to which THEY curtsy slightly)

Good day, Maisy. Good day, Daisy. Very good to see y'all. I... My Mama and I, really appreciate all your kindnesses to Daddy in his illness.

DAISY MAY

Well, Lorenzo, we've known your family all our lives and our two daddy's were such good friends when they were both alive that we just wanted to do anything we could to help your mama.

MAISY DAY

The funeral was so beautiful and we were so happy to see you and your son again and we wanted to drop by and bring some solace for the body in this time of sorrow ...

DAISY MAY

I made collards straight out of my garden—

MAISY DAY

—picked them this morning—

DAISY MAY

—and somma' those juicy neck bones that your daddy loved. And I made apple pie—

MAISY DAY

—and I made a chocolate cake.

(trying to upstage DAISY MAY)

I remembered it was your favorite.

DAISY MAY

(competing with HER sister for HIS attention) Oh, no, sista' you are quite mistaken. Lorenzo's favorite was always apple pie. Wasn't it, Lornezo?

MAISY DAY

No, it weren't. His favorite was always chocolate double layer cake, usta' be called German chocolate cake, remember? (shows cake).

LORENZO

Well, ladies, ladies, I love them both ... very much. And this is so thoughtful of y'all ...

MARY ALICE

I'll just leave you three alone for a while.

LORENZO

Mama? (beat, looks uncomfortable) Wait. (can't think what to say) Don't forget to come back, now. We scheduled reading the will for later. Jalani and Eva will be back from downtown soon and we all have to head back to New York tomorrow.

MARY ALICE

(exiting)

Yes, dear. Don't you worry.

MAISY DAY

Leaving so soon, Lorenzo?

LORENZO

Yes, Daisy—

MAISY DAY

Maisy—

LORENZO

Oh, so sorry, Maisy.

MAISY DAY

Oh, we get that all the time being twins and all.

DAISY MAY

And who is Eva? Have you finally met someone?

LORENZO

Eva, oh no, Eva is Jalani's girlfriend. It was really sweet of her to come down with us.

DAISY MAY

Oh good. (beat) I mean isn't that nice. So you are still single.

LORENZO

Yes, ma'am. You know I'm just too busy to date or be in a relationship or anything ... like that. And I do still miss Berneice—

MAISY DAY

Berneice was a lovely lady, Lorenzo.

DAISY MAY

We so liked Berneice and we grieved so when we heard she had passed.

MAISY DAY

That must have been hard for you, Lorenzo, after so many years of marriage.

LORENZO

Thirteen years. She was much too young to die.

DAISY MAY

Much too young.

MAISY DAY

Much too young. But none of us are gettin' any younger either.

DAISY MAY

No, indeed, and we have to get on with our lives.

MAISY DAY

They say New York is sooo busy.

DAISY MAY

So dirty, I hear.

MAISY DAY

So noisy, too.

DAISY MAY

And sooo full of people you don't really meet anyone ... special.

MAISY DAY

That's why we love Birmingham, still a city with such a nice small town feel and people are so warm and outgoing ...

    (SHE moves to the couch to sit beside LORENZO and gives
       HIM the pie which he puts down on his lap)

People here have known each other all their lives—

DAISY MAY

(going to sit on the other side of LORENZO on the couch)

—just like we have ... always known each other and all the people in the community.

MAISY DAY

They've grown up together—

DAISY MAY

—just like we have ... When we were kids we played together, went to the same school, the same church. (smiling)

MAISY DAY

They kinda know each other ... what they like ... what they need (smiling)

DAISY MAY

What they like ... and what they need.

LORENZO

(increasingly uncomfortable) I'm sure they do.

MAISY DAY

And we know people shouldn't be alone.

DAISY MAY

Yes. Sadly we've been alone for a long time—

MAISY DAY

Together—

DAISY MAY

alone ... together. Since Papa died. Of course, Mama died first ... but then there was Papa and he was sick a long, long time—

MAISY DAY

And he needed us—

DAISY MAY

—couldn't do without us—

LORENZO

I'm sure—

MAISY DAY

It was hard—

DAISY MAY

—hard ... very hard for the both of us.

MAISY DAY

—to put our needs aside and serve our daddy, night—

DAISY MAY

—and day. For seven long years that the good Lord gave Daddy.

MAISY DAY

Night—

DAISY MAY

—and day—

MAISY DAY

Cooking—

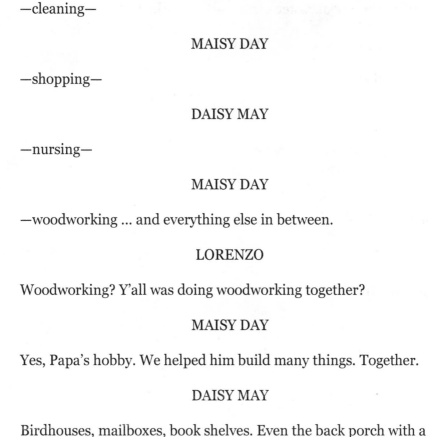

DAISY MAY

—cleaning—

MAISY DAY

—shopping—

DAISY MAY

—nursing—

MAISY DAY

—woodworking ... and everything else in between.

LORENZO

Woodworking? Y'all was doing woodworking together?

MAISY DAY

Yes, Papa's hobby. We helped him build many things. Together.

DAISY MAY

Birdhouses, mailboxes, book shelves. Even the back porch with a swing for us to swing together.

MAISY DAY

We have real nice book shelves. You should see them. Come over if you have time before you go.

DAISY MAY

Yes, you got to come see them.

MAISY DAY

Beautiful book shelves ... in his den. In my bedroom—

DAISY MAY

—and my bedroom, sister … right above my bed.

LORENZO

I'm sure they're lovely.

MAISY DAY

Oh they are. And so feminine.

DAISY MAY

Such fine detail.

MAISY DAY

Intricate, Daddy said.

DAISY MAY

Fine detail. Daddy had an eye for detail—

MAISY DAY

—and an eye for the ladies, Sister, don't forget the ladies.

DAISY MAY

How could I forget. It was the only thing Mama and Daddy ever argued about.

MAISY DAY

Our mama was very jealous, Lorenzo.

DAISY MAY

How could she not be. He was such a fine figure of a man. Like you, Lorenzo.

MAISY DAY

Oh yes, like you Lorenzo, handsome..smart. So big—

DAISY MAY

—so strong—

MAISY DAY

—so ... big.

DAISY MAY

That was the only thing they ever argued about.

MAISY DAY

But they argued so often, sister.

DAISY MAY

So much jealousy—

MAISY DAY

—the yelling

DAISY MAY

—pounding the walls

MAISY DAY

Once I saw Mama slap Daddy.

DAISY MAY

I never saw that.

MAISY DAY

I did, Sister, it was a terrible thing. Maybe you were out ... some-
where. But I was there. They were yelling. It was about some
woman ... like always ... and then Mama just slapped him. Hard.
I heard it all the way up in my bedroom and I came running

35

down the stairs. I saw Mama crying. And Daddy standing there surprised, holding his hand back as if he were about to hit her in return and there ... was ... this big red mark on his face and I knew Mama had slapped him really hard.

DAISY MAY

It was bound to happen. All those fights. It seemed like we never had any peace in that house when Mama was alive ... Rest her soul.

MAISY DAY

Rest her soul ... Mama was a good woman, Lorenzo.

DAISY MAY

A good woman ... But a jealous woman.

MAISY DAY

With good reason.

DAISY MAY

Papa had a wandering eye, that's for sure. But when Mama passed Daddy finally calmed down.

MAISY DAY

He missed her something terrible.

DAISY MAY

There was never another woman again. He got real quiet. And then our house was peaceable. Like yours, Lorenzo.

MAISY DAY

Yes, Lorenzo, your parents always seemed ... calm.

DAISY MAY

Peaceable.

MAISY DAY

Loving.

DAISY MAY

We envied that, Lorenzo.

MAISY DAY

Your folks never fought that we could hear.

LORENZO

No, I don't think I ever heard them fight or even raise their voices to each other.

MAISY DAY

No ... well ... there was ... one time—

DAISY MAY

That one time was something.

MAISY DAY

That was something.

DAISY MAY

So out of character

.

MAISY DAY

I was really shocked to hear them yelling at each other. And everyone could hear all up and down the block. Such a carrying on...and about a box of all silly things.

LORENZO

I never heard anything about a box. What box?

MAISY DAY

Maybe you were away at college?

DAISY MAY

You might have been at college. We were so proud when you got your degree.

MAISY DAY

And summa cumma summa too. We were all very proud. Summa, something—

DAISY MAY

Summa cum louder, sister, louder than just plain old summa.

LORENZO

You said they argued over a box?

DAISY MAY

Oh it was some argument. The yelling and shouting. Doors slamming. Your mama crying.

MAISY DAY

We kept hearing Mary Alice yell: "Throw it away, Eddie. Just throw it away, throw that box away."

DAISY MAY

"Throw the damn thing away" pardon my French, Lorenzo, but that's what she said. I can still hear Mary Alice yelling, and crying, and carrying on.

MAISY DAY

And then it was over. And we never heard about it again.

DAISY MAY

Never knew what set it off. Never heard another word about it again.

MAISY DAY

Never heard your mama yell again either. Never another fight.

DAISY MAY

Like our house after our mama passed. Quiet, peaceable. And now Papa's gone and it's real ... real ... quiet.

MAISY DAY

A peaceful house ... and quiet.

DAISY MAY

Too quiet.

MAISY DAY

Too quiet maybe.

DAISY MAY

But now we're free.

MAISY DAY

Free of the burden of taking care of Papa. (beat) No more making birdhouses—

DAISY MAY

—or bookshelves. It's like Juneteenth all over again.

MAISY DAY

You know Sister, that always seemed so funny, those dumbass nigras in Texas not gettin' word of the Emancipation Proclamation for two and a half years after old Abe Lincoln signed it. Then for weeks they didn't know that the South had surrendered and they was free. When the war ended they finally heard the news like it just happened that very minute.

DAISY MAY

They heard the news and just laid down their sacks of cotton, just left their tools in the fields and walked away.

MAISY DAY

Walked out of them fields and never looked back. 'Cause they was free.

DAISY MAY

That's kinda' how it was for us.

MAISY DAY

Like the Emancipation Proxamation. The locks fell off the jail-house doors

DAISY MAY

Whatever word you choose … we're free.

MAISY DAY

Our servitude is ended. No longer—

DAISY MAY

—we are no longer slaves to another human being.

MAISY DAY

Free to follow our own dreams now—

DAISY MAY

—to satisfy our own needs now.

LORENZO

(as they move closer) Oh.

MAISY DAY

People have needs. We all do. You do, Lorenzo. You know you do. You shouldn't be alone.

DAISY MAY

You shouldn't. It's not natural, not for a man ... not for a woman neither.

LORENZO

Well, I'm not alone ... here's Jalani ... my work ... my students. I keep busy.

MAISY DAY

But at the end of the day, Lorenzo—

DAISY MAY

—when you come home—

MAISY DAY

—tired—

DAISY MAY

—spent—

MAISY DAY

—alone

DAISY MAY

—all alone—

MAISY DAY

And all you want is—

DAISY MAY

—a warm hand to hold yours—(SHE holds HIS hand)

MAISY DAY

—a soft shoulder to lay your head on … (SHE moves HIS head to HER shoulder)

DAISY MAY

—and pie

MAISY DAY

—oh yes, pie … we got pie. Hot pie (LORENZO starts, MAISY DAY's hand slips) Oh. (beat) I seem to have my fingers in your pie. (She lifts HER fingers covered with pie filling)

LORENZO

I'm sorry … Oh, my goodness. I am so sorry.

DAISY MAY

(drawing a tissue from HER purse) No, no, nothing to worry about. Just a little apple on the finga'. See. (offers HER sister's fingers to LORENZO as if he might lick them)

LORENZO

(HE leans in a moment as if ready to lick Maisy's finger himself but then catches himself and jumps up) Well, pie is great. Pie is … (beat) really, really great. I can't thank you … both for baking a special pie … and … cake … for me, (to MAISY) Daisy—

MAISY

Maisy

LORENZO

Maisy. (to DAISY) Daisy ... I can't thank y'all, enough for this. It's a great treat. A great treat. Let me just make sure you get back home nice and clean. (HE takes the tissue to wipe HER hands, calling to offstage) Mama! Mama! Could you come ... help! Mama!

MARY ALICE

(enters immediately as if SHE has been just outside listening) Oh my, what has been happening here. Are you all right Maisy Day?

DAISY MAY

Of course, just a little accident.

MAISY DAY

Well, we must be going.

DAISY MAY

Yes, going.

LORENZO

Well, you were so kind. So kind to bring me ... pies. Thank you (to MAISY) Daisy May.

MAISY DAY

Maisy.

LORENZO

Yes, yes indeed. Thank you so much.

(all exit stage right to kitchen and front door. We hear doors open and close. We hear offstage:)

LORENZO

Goodbye Maisy.

DAISY MAY

Daisy.

LORENZO

Oh. Good to see y'all. Goodbye to ... both of you.

(MARY ALICE and LORENZO reenter shortly)

LORENZO

Oh my god, Mama. How could you leave me alone with those two.

MARY ALICE

Oh, don't dramatize, Son. They're very nice ladies, Lorenzo.

LORENZO

More like hungry cats—and I was the mouse.

MARY ALICE

Well, you're still a handsome man, Son. You still attract some feminine interest. Berneice has been gone a long time and you grieved and we all miss her. But it's time you were married again and I wouldn't wait too long if I were you ... Time passes. You wake up one day and you're alone again ... and that Maisy Day is a fine woman ... and a good cook ... and easy to look at too. (long beat) I ... I miss Eddie (whimpers) ... so much. (cries)

LORENZO

I know you do Mama.

MARY ALICE

(HE helps HER to sit on the couch. Long beat as SHE takes deep breaths. SHE appears worried)

You know, Son, I had the strangest dream last night. I dreamed I was back 30 years. They had just bombed the Baptist Church on 16th street. There was smoke and sirens. I couldn't see clearly. A woman, a Black woman, she was a woman, but she wasn't dressed right, you know, like she wasn't from here, but she looked familiar. She stepped up and gave me a little girl's black shoe. (beat). I took it but when I looked down it was covered in blood. A little girl's blood it must have been.

LORENZO

Those were evil days, Mama.

MARY ALICE

Killing children. Lord have mercy! Who would ever have thought it would come to that.

LORENZO

I was in Atlanta when it happened. But I knew one of those girls, Addie Mae Collins. I went to high school with her brother. She was only 14—

MARY ALICE

To think some White man would kill innocent little girls 'cause they were Black. Those were evil days, Lorenzo, but that's passed. Why am I dreaming about those old times now? Don't I have enough pain without evil dreams of evil times.

LORENZO

It's just a dream, Mama, don't you worry about it. They used to call this city Bombingham but that's all in the past. Don't worry about it, Mama, those days are gone. Gone and forgotten.

MARY ALICE

I haven't forgotten, Son. I can never forget.

LORENZO

(long pause, changing the subject) You know, I always wondered ... why Maisy ... is White ... I could never figure that out.

MARY ALICE

Why Daisy is White, you mean? Well, Daisy ain't White. She may seem lighter in skin tone than Maisy but they are twins, Lorenzo. She is Black, sweetie. Lot of those Bensens coulda passed for White. Daisy's great Aunt June looked Whiter than Jalani's little White girl friend ... what's her name?

LORENZO

Eva. Jalanai's girlfriend is Eva.

MARY ALICE

(Dismissive) Anyway ... as I was saying, Aunt June lived up in Chicago for years passing as White and those Northern White folk never knew it.

LORENZO

But how is that possible?

MARY ALICE

It's all possible with slavery, sweetie. I guess not possible but inevitable, even. Pretty Black women working at the plantation, no Black man around to protect them ... there's always going to be a White boy in the woodpile. Leaves a stain ... a mark of shame on our race. That Daisy never seemed right to me. Like her White skin made her better than us or somethin'.

LORENZO

She seemed nice to me, Mama.

MARY ALICE

White is as White does—and White always does us wrong, Son. But her sister is a real sweet woman, Lorenzo, you should be thinking about Maisy.

LORENZO

Hmmm. When the Bensen sisters and me were talking, Mama. They mentioned something about a box.

MARY ALICE

A box?

LORENZO

They said something about you and Papa arguing over a box. Made it sound like quite a fight ... arguing ... yelling.

MARY ALICE

That's just crazy. Those two ladies have been alone too long. They're hearing things. I never argued with your father in my life. Not once. About a box? A box? That's ridiculous.

(SHE rises and exits hurriedly, leaving LORENZO alone)

END SCENE 2

ACT 1

SCENE 3

AT RISE: We hear the sound of jungle birds. Projections of native huts in West Africa, of women in indigenous clothing, everyday life in a village.

ALICE/AFENYI enters carrying a heavy jar. SHE places it down carefully before a projection of a hut. SHE looks around. SHE begins preparing a fire as for cooking. We hear drumming. The scene is idyllic. Lights out.

Act 1

SCENE 4

AT RISE: In the same parlor in the Pace house but later that same day. EVA BARNES is sitting in a chair as JALANI PACE absent-mindedly looks through the roll top desk, opening and closing drawers. SHE is wrapped in a colorful, homemade quilt.

EVA

You o.k.?

JALANI

(Not paying much attention to EVA) Yeah. Feeling a little cooped up is all. Birmingham is not a happening place, baby. Even down-town was pretty dead. Looks like most of the businesses have left. That downtown looks like a big ghetto.

EVA

I don't know I really liked those civil rights memorials in the park, the one of the police dogs attacking the marchers and the one of the four little girls killed in that church bombing across the street.

JALANI

Yeah, that stuff's o.k. but I'm ready to head back up north. You see a town like this and you really appreciate a big city like New York where something's always going on. (beat) What are you reading?

EVA

Oh, something I found in your granddad's bookcase. He had a lot of books. Old ones, mostly. And I love these quilts. They are so pretty.

JALANI

Big Momma has been making those all her life. For years I hung onto the one she made me as a baby. I even named that quilt. I think I was still taking it to bed with me when I was ten—

EVA

You named your quilt?

JALANI

Yeah.

EVA

Well?

JALANI

I called it 'Lamby.'

EVA

'Lamby?'

JALANI

Big Momma had stitched in a picture of a little lamb ... Well, I was only ten.

EVA

No, I think it's cute.

JALANI

I took 'Lamby' everywhere. I slept with her every night ... until it finally just fell apart. Whenever I see a beautiful quilt I think of Big Momma.

EVA

What are you looking for in that desk?

JALANI

Nothing. Just killing time till Dad and Big Momma get done with the neighbors. Who knew that a funeral was such a big two day social event, huh? (turns) What's the book?

EVA

(Reading the spine) *American Slave Narratives*

JALANI

That must be a million years old. I didn't even know slaves could read or write. You know, 'tote that bale,' 'chop that cotton, yes, massa,' no, massa'

EVA

Just listen to this: 'Slavery was the worst days was ever seed in the world. They was things past tellin', but I got the scars on my old body to show to this day. I seed worse than what happened to me. I seed them put the men and women in the stock with they hands screwed down through holes in the board and they feets tied together and they naked behinds to the world. Solomon the overseer beat them with a big whip and massa' look on. The n-'s better not stop in the fields when they hear them yellin'. They cut the flesh most to the bones and some they was taken them out of the stocks and put them on the beds, they never got up again.'

JALANI

Jesus! Jesus! Did that really happen? Who could do that to someone?

EVA

When a n- died they let his folks come outta the fields to see him afore he died. They buried him the same day, take a big plank and bust it with a ax in the middle 'nough to bend it back, and put the dead n- in betwixt it. They'd cart them down to the graveyard and not bury them deep 'nough that buzzards wouldn't come circlin' round. N-'s mourns now, but in them days they wasn't no time for mournin'.

JALANI

That's cold ... just stone cold.

EVA

"Mary Reynolds, a slave ... right here in Alabama, gave this testimony in 1931 at the age of 100."

JALANI

(Comes over and kneels beside EVA. Takes the book out of her hands and puts it down. Takes HER hands in HIS. Puts on an imagined slave/southern dialect.) Those days are gone, baby ... but I be your slave. A little shuffle, step and fetch-it. Nothing too good for the massa's young ... (touching HER arm) pure, alabaster white daughter. You the image of everything I'm not suppose to touch. Back in the day they woulda hung me like a dog from a tree for touching a White girl.

EVA

Jelly. (ruffling his hair). My Jelly Roll.

JALANI

Once you had Black you can't never go back.

(JALANI and EVA maneuver to the couch in a clinch and are about to move into some serious kissing and petting.)

LORENZO

(entering the room, seeing the romantic tableau, clearing throat) Ahem. What's up y'all? What are y'all doing?

(JALANI jumps to his feet. EVA pretends to read her book)

JALANI

Nothing, Pops. Just having a little fun. (Turns HIS back to HIS father to straighten HIS clothes)

LORENZO

Have either of you seen Mama's glasses? (HE crosses to desk and looks around, does the same at a table) She can't see a damn thing without those glasses and she keeps losing them.

EVA

I thought I saw them in the kitchen, Mr. Pace.

LORENZO

I'll look there next, I guess. Watcha' reading?

EVA

(she offers him the book) *American Slave Narratives.*

(HE takes book, looks at it briefly)

Lots of old books in the bookcase.

LORENZO

Dad was a reader all his life, that's for sure. A real history buff, especially around the South and slavery. I don't know why he was so interested in that stuff. I never got into it. I remember this book though. This is bad stuff. If I read this it just makes me angry. It makes me want to hate all White people for what they did to my people. (gives book back to her) All about how overseers whipped the slaves to the bone but never broke their spirit. Brave people, I know that, but that history is all messed up. It makes me ashamed to think they could do that to us and we couldn't fight back, couldn't protect our families, our women. You don't need to read this, Eva. We just need to put it away and forget it. (HE takes the book from HER and puts it back on a shelf. He picks up another book, reads the cover title) *The Theology of Thomas Aquinas.* Jalani, however, you should read a lot more if you're expecting to go to Morehouse next year.

(Tosses the book to JALANI)

JALANI

(JALANI stops fiddling with a pen at the desk and catches the book) Yes, Dad.

LORENZO

I'll see if those glasses are in the kitchen. She can't see anything without them.

(HE exits. JALANI puts the book aside without interest)

EVA

Morehouse? I thought you were going to NYU with me? Morehouse is in Atlanta, like a million miles away.

JALANI

Nah, it's just like 900 miles from Manhattan, I checked. Dad went
to Morehouse. Gramps went to Morehouse. Now they say I have
to. I don't want to go down there. Believe me, this n- doesn't want
to live in the old Southern swamps with them peckerwoods, red-
necks and hicks. I'm a city boy.

EVA

When were you going to tell me?

JALANI

I don't know. After the funeral, I guess.

EVA

The funeral was yesterday.

JALANI

So I told you today.

EVA

No, you didn't, your dad told me today.

JALANI

I was planning to tell you today.

EVA

You know I can't go ... it's all male ... and Black.

JALANI

I know. But I'll come home once a month. We can be together
every summer. We can get jobs out at the beach at Coney Island or

at the Natural History Museum on the West Side. Then we can be together every day. A little nookie in the basement with the mummies ... Would you like that? (HE tries to tickle HER)

EVA

Cut that out. You know it won't work. We'll just drift apart. I thought we had something special.

JALANI

We do ... we have ... we will. Look, I tried to talk to Dad about this Morehouse thing but he gets kinda scary on the subject. He's into this family tradition. The whole Pace family saga and all. And that means college and a profession with a title just like every other Pace.

EVA

You're afraid of him, aren't you?

JALANI

Nah. (Beat) Well, (Beat) Yeah. He is scary. His mind's made up. The whole Pace ... (makes air quotation makes around word 'Pace') ... name thing is important to him.

EVA

But look at what happened. Your father didn't become a minister like his father and grandfather. He's an artist and a teacher. He didn't stay in the South. He came to New York City. He became his own man and he's still a Pace (adds quotation marks around 'Pace'), isn't he?

JALANI

Yeah, I guess.

EVA

Are you going to be a slave? (gets up and retrieves slavery book from shelf) Are you? There are many kinds of slaves. Are you going to be a slave to tradition? to names, even if it limits you as a person? You have to be your own man, Jalani, just like your dad was. He followed his heart. You follow yours.

JALANI

Yeah. But you don't understand this whole name thing. Pace has to stand for something special. It has for a hundred years or more. Names are like ... labels ... like definitions ... they're who you are.

EVA

But your dad's name is Lorenzo.

JALANI

Yeah, so?

EVA

Lorenzo Pace. Sounds Italian to me.

JALANI

We ain't Italian.

EVA

There's Black Irish, maybe there's Black (with exaggerated accent) Eyetalians?

JALANI

I don't think so.

EVA

So where'd that come from?

JALANI

I don't know. Granddad was Eddie and that's American and I'm Jalani and that's African.

EVA

So, who are you? I'm a Barnes, right and that means nothing to me. I'm just me, Eva. You're just Jalani, my Jelly Roll.

(THEY hug. HE pulls away)

JALANI

Wait a minute, your family name means nothing to you?

EVA

No, absolutely nothing ... because it's not my name.

JALANI

What? Are you some kind of spy ... a criminal on the lam? Is Barnes an alias?

EVA

Well, sorta. My great grandfather was Andrzej Barnovski, a Jewish peddler from Poland. He was running from the anti-semites and the pogroms. Some-how he got from Krakow to America. He got off the ship at Ellis Island, may-be 1880, 1881 ... So he walks up to the immigration table with a single beat-up suitcase he sewed together filled with all his worldly goods. And this big, burly, red faced Irish immigration officer asks him his name. At least that's how my grandfather tells the story, when my Dad's not around. Dad doesn't want to hear anything about the old country ... or Jews for that matter. Anyway this fat, greasy, Irish 'mick,' (air quotes) my granddad's words, leans over, with the smell of corned beef and cabbage mixed with Irish whiskey on his breath, and says 'what's your name, you stinkin' Kike?'
And great granddad says 'Andrzej ... Andrzej Barnovski,' but he says it in this little quavery voice, because he barely knows English and he's afraid they're gonna send him back to Poland on the next ship. The guy sitting there, the Irishman, but more importantly the Irish-American, says 'speak up you filthy Yid, I didn't hear you.'
And great granddad says 'Andrzej Barnovski,' a little louder this time. 'That's not an American name,' says the Irishman. 'You're an American now. From now on you're not Andrzej, ... you're Andrew and you're not Barnovski ... you're Barnes' . You're Andrew Barnes ... ' and he was from that day forward. And he named his sons Andrew and John and Steven. And Steven named his daughter, me, Eva. So my name is a fraud. An invention to blend in. Barnes is pretty spiffy, upper crust even, I like it o.k. ... but it's a fake. In America we make our own traditions. We're free. We're not slaves

57

... to names, ... or Dads ... or traditions. Stand up to him, Jalani, if you want to be with me.

JALANI

That's easy for you to say. You don't know how my dad can be when his mind's made up.

MARY ALICE
(shouting from off stage) Jalani!

(JALANI doesn't answer but HE seems to get an idea)
(the shouting sounds closer)
Jalani!

JALANI

(to EVA) Tell you what, Missy 'stand up to him, if you want to be with me.' I'll stand up to Pops if you stand up to Big Mama.

EVA

What? What are you talking about?

JALANI

C'mon Eva. You know what I mean. Big Momma hasn't exactly taken a liking to you.

EVA

Well, she does seem a little standoffish. What's that about?

JALANI

Hell if I know but I suggest that if YOU want to be with ME, then you should find out and fix it because if Big Momma ain't happy, ain't nobody happy.

EVA

Exactly what are you saying, Jalani?

JALANI

What I'm saying is I'll stand up to Pops about this college thing if
you stand up to Big Momma about why she seems to dislike you
when she hardly even knows you.

EVA

OK, Buster, she doesn't scare me. It's a deal.

(SHE sticks out her hand to shake on the deal and HE pulls HER
in for a kiss)

MARY ALICE

(entering) Has anyone seen my glasses?

(JALANI and EVA pull apart)

JALANI

No ma'am.

EVA

Mr. Pace is looking for them in the kitchen, Mrs. Pace.

MARY ALICE

I don't know where I put anything anymore. If Eddie was here he'd
tell me I'd forget my nose on my face if it wasn't attached. Eddie...
Eddie (speaking to the air) Why'd you go and leave me, Eddie,
sweetheart?

EVA

(tries to hug MARY ALICE) I'm so sorry for your loss, Mrs. Pace,
so sorry.

MARY ALICE

(pulls away from EVA) Hold on now little girl. I don't need your
pity. I'll be all right. Six months of illness and 80 years old. He was
just ready, that's all, he was just ready. I'm ready too.

JALANI

We all miss him, Big Momma. (beat) Big Momma, could I talk to you about something? (gives EVA a meaningful look)

EVA

(SHE looks puzzled, then gets it) Let me go help Mr. Pace look for your glasses in the kitchen.

MARY ALICE

Hold on a minute, girl. Is that my quilt you all wrapped up in?

EVA

Yes, ma'am. It's beautiful.

MARY ALICE

Take it off this instant ... (MARY ALICE reaches for the quilt and practically rips it off EVA's shoulders) I don't want nothing happening to it. Who told you to help yourself to my quilt anyway? Don't you know only family is allowed to have my quilts?

EVA

Mrs. Pace. I'm so so sorry. I didn't mean to—

MARY ALICE

Just put it away and put it away now! And don't you ever touch another thing in this house without asking first, you low class ... Do you understand me?

EVA

(Looks bewildered and hurt). Yes. Ma'am. (EVA is crying. SHE slips past Mary Alice and exits)

JALANI

(Flustered) Big Momma, I can't believe what you just ... What ... what—

MARY ALICE

Spit it out, boy. Come on.

JALANI

Look at what you just did. Eva didn't mean any harm. What was that all about?

MARY ALICE

(looks off to kitchen where EVA exited) Uh oh. I'm not getting into a discussion with you over that little White girl. Why did you bring her into this house? This is the South, boy. White folks stay with their kind. We stay with ours. White folks is still White folks and they don't like n-'s messing with their White girls. You gonna wind up dead just like what they did to that little Emmet Till boy.

JALANI

Emmet who? What's he got to do with Eva?

MARY ALICE

Emmet Till, a 14 year old Black boy who come down to Mississippi from Chicago. He didn't know the rules down here either. Maybe he whistled at a White girl and maybe he didn't but they took him out one night an' gouged out his eyes, cut off his privates, wrapped him in barbed wire and threw him in the river. When they found his mangled body the funeral director wanted to have his funeral with a closed casket but his mama said, 'No, you open it up right here in church. Let everyone see what they did to my baby.'

JALANI

I bet that was a long time ago.

MARY ALICE

40 years ago, boy, but somethings don't ever change in the South.

JALANI

That was then and this is now Big Mama. Nobody cares about that stuff anymore. Eva is cool. We go to the same school. We have the same friends, white and black ... brown ... all kinds of people from around the world. Besides, dad really likes her.

MARY ALICE

(sounds skeptical) Oh, so Lorenzo likes her does he?

JALANI

Yeah. That's not the problem, Big Momma. No, it's more about where I go to college—

MARY ALICE

Morehouse.

JALANI

Yeah, well that's the thing ... maybe Morehouse ain't for me. Maybe that's just Dad's idea, not mine.

MARY ALICE

Your granddad went to Morehouse.

JALANI

Yeah, but—

MARY ALICE

His daddy went to Morehouse—

JALANI

Yeah, but—

MARY ALICE

Your Daddy went to Morehouse—

JALANI

Yeah, but—

MARY ALICE

And that ain't good enough for you, boy?

JALANI

Sure, sure, Big Momma. Morehouse is great ... and all, but—

MARY ALICE

They opened that school right after the Civil War ended. One of
the first schools where a Black man could get an education and
become something in this country.

JALANI

Yeah, but ... it's all guys, Big Momma, and all Black and—

MARY ALICE

You bet it's all Black. Black boys becoming men and college graduates and doctors and lawyers with no help from any White folks.
(beat) Oh, I get it. That's where she comes in ... (with a nod of her
head towards the kitchen) ... is that what it is? The White girl?

JALANI

I love her, Big Momma. I can't go to school and leave her behind
for four years. I love her ... just like you and gramps did.

MARY ALICE

Oh, boy do not compare that ... that ... little ... White, Jew girl to
my Eddie!

JALANI

Sorry Big Momma ... but love is love and we all want someone very
special in our life. If you had it, you understand what I want.

63

MARY ALICE

You think it comes easy? You think four years apart ... at college ... is hard? You don't know hard, boy. Hard is not having the money to go to college. Hard is deciding between buying a meal and buying a textbook. And it ain't just about money. You think you love that White girl?

JALANI

Eva, Big Momma, her name is Eva, not 'White girl,' ... and I do love her.

MARY ALICE

And you think the White girl loves you?

JALANI

I know she does. I was thinking maybe you could talk to Pops about Morehouse ... you know, help me convince him I could go to a school closer to home.

MARY ALICE

Then you're a fool and it don't matter where you go to college because you don't have the sense God gave a mule to learn anything anyway, boy.

JALANI

I'm gonna graduate top of my class just like Daddy did.

MARY ALICE

Yeah, but your daddy had the sense to marry your momma, a good Black girl from a good Christian home. He didn't go sniffing after White girls like you.

JALANI

Big Momma, I never heard you talk like this before, so hung up on color. That's old talk. You need to change.

MARY ALICE

Who needs to change, boy?

JALANI

You do. That's all in the past. Nobody cares about that today. I've got White friends, I've got Indian friends, Mexican friends, Jewish friends, Muslim friends. You name it. New York is not Birmingham and 1991 is not the 1950's. The civil rights fight is done and over. We won!

MARY ALICE

Who won, boy? Some things change and some things don't. All I know is Black people have no business living with White people. You think they're nice, some White people because they smile and talk about equality? You think they love you, some Jewish girl, because she's into what, affirmative action, diversity? Or maybe she just likes showing off a Black boyfriend to her Jewish friends for a while. She'll take you home to some nice matzo ball soup, dance a 'hora' in their living room, and meet her parents just to have fun scaring them, show how liberal she is. Guess who's come to dinner? You think you're Sidney Portier? (beat) She's not gonna marry you.

JALANI

That's just sick, Big Momma.

MARY ALICE

Believe me, White people are only looking for ways to bring you down and hurt you. I warn you, Jalani, no good can come to Black people from any White people in this whole country, north or south ... east or west. First they killed all the Indians and took their land. Then they brought our people from Africa and worked them to death. This country is OF White people, BY White people, and most importantly, FOR White people. Always has been. Always will be. They won, boy, they won ... we didn't.

JALANI

But you have White friends. I saw White people at grampa's funeral.

MARY ALICE

They're White people. They're not friends. Not people you turn
your back on. Not people you trust and not people you tell your
secrets to. White people can be o.k. if they stay where they are and
leave us be where we are. If they stay out of our business and leave
us alone. Jalani, how many White people you think have ever been
in this parlor in the time Eddie and I were together?

JALANI

I don't know. 50? 60?

MARY ALICE

Two. Just two. In 57 years. Two. A banker from the Morgan Bank
who came to try to foreclose on your granddad after the war. And
the Sheriff of Birmingham who came in here to ask Bishop Pace
not to stand with those northern Freedom Riders in the 60's and
try to keep Birmingham quiet after the church bombing. Money
and fear that's only things move White people to enter a Black
man's home. Not neither one of them would sit down in our chairs
or take a cup of tea from my kitchen. Just wanted to say their piece
and get out of a Black house as quick as they can without any of
the black rubbing off on them.

JALANI

Make it three.

MARY ALICE

Hunh?

JALANI

Three White people have been in this parlor. Eva. She sits down
here in your chairs. She sleeps in your bed. She eats from your
kitchen. She ain't afraid of any black rubbing off on her.

MARY ALICE

Maybe that's how it seems to you, Jalani, but White people don't
change their color. If they're here they want something and it is
not something good for us. I don't trust them. I never have and I
never will.

JALANI

Wow, you really seem to hate on White people, Big Momma. What did they do to you? Why do you hate them?

MARY ALICE

Why you say that? They didn't do nothin' to me. I don't hate anyone, Jalani. The Good Lord taught us not to hate. I just know to keep my distance and my eyes open. And you better watch out too.

JALANI

Times have changed, Big Momma, and we gotta change with them.

LORENZO

(Entering from kitchen, holding old pair of glasses in HIS hand. EVA follows)

I found them. (Beat) Well, Eva found them.

EVA

They were in the fridge.

LORENZO

In the vegetable drawer of all places. Mama, how did you leave your glasses there?

MARY ALICE

(getting agitated) I don't know, boy. I can't remember everything I do. I can't. I just can't. Eddie gone. Times changing. I just can't! (SHE seems on the verge of tears)

LORENZO

Mama, maybe we should do this another day.

MARY ALICE

(to LORENZO) No, I know you have to get back to New York City and all that crazy city bus-yness. (beat) Let's just get it over with.

(takes HER glasses and puts them on. The doorbell rings). Would you get that, Jalani?

(JALANI exits)

LORENZO

Mama, we're not going back to New York alone, you're coming with us.

(JALANI reenters with DAISY MAY who has yet another pie)

MARY ALICE

Don't start that again, Lorenzo. After all these beautiful years in this house, I am not leaving my home ...

(ALL turn to see DAISY MAY)

DAISY MAY

Well, Maisy was out to her woodworking class and I got to thinking we was wrong and it was peach pie that was Lorenzo's favorite not chocolate or apple and so I done baked another ... (SHE stops realizing SHE has entered at a bad time. Looks from face to face.) ... maybe another time would be more ... opportune.

MARY ALICE

No, no, you come in gal and have a seat. Lorenzo take this beautiful pie.

(HE steps forward to take pie. DAISY MAY sits. When HE returns
            LORENZO sits near HER. SHE smiles at HIM)

We were just having a little quiet discussion here about how I am quite capable of living in my own house by my own self.

LORENZO

(Looking uncomfortable in DAISY MAY's presence) Thank you for the new pie, Daisy.

DAISY MAY

(SHE beams because HE has gotten her name right at last) Dais
... oh, you got it right ... You are so welcome, Lorenzo.

LORENZO

(Turing again to MARY ALICE) You need help, Mama. We want
you to live with us in peace and comfort.

JALANI

We do, Grams. We want to make sure you are well taken care of.

MARY ALICE

I'm not going anywhere.

LORENZO

What if you fall and break a leg? Who'd find you? Who would be
here to help you get up? ... Who's going to buy groceries for you?
And do everything to take care of this big house?

JALANI

Who'll find your glasses ... if not Eva?

LORENZO

Who'll take you to church? I don't want you down here all alone.
I'd never be able to stop worrying about you.

MARY ALICE

Mrs. Wilson will do my shopping just like she did for your daddy
and me. There must be ten sister—friends down at your daddy's
church that will take me to services every Sunday. You'll take me,
won't you Daisy, dear?

DAISY

Of course I will sista' Mary Alice.

MARY ALICE

And I don't fall. And I can find my own glasses ... without the help of ... Eva.

DAISY MAY

(Realizing that SHE may be on the wrong side of LORENZO) Of course ... (THEY all turn to look at HER. SHE is embarrassed) ... of course, Daddy wouldn't have been able to get along without the two of us. I'm not saying Miz Pace that you're old or anything like that but Lorenzo's just trying to help, I'm sure. He just wants what's best for you.

LORENZO

That's right, Mama, you are coming with us. I told Daddy that I'd take care of you and I will. That was the one thing on his mind at the end. I swore to him with all my heart and soul I'd take care of you. And that's that, now!

MARY ALICE

And how do I leave my home? ... and my friends? ... and our church? How can I not go to church on Sundays and still see Eddie in my mind right up there in the pulpit. Tall and straight in his shining black robe.

That was the first place I saw him. Must be more than 60 years ago now. I don't remember a word he said that day. I just remember that he was the handsomest man I ever saw. I was 15 that day my parents brought me but I remember. I thought 'Now I've seen God' ... because he had God in him. I couldn't take my eyes off him. He shone with beauty ... and love.

(EVA moves close and slips HER hand in JALANI's. DAISY MAY looks at LORENZO)

I couldn't talk to him after the service. He shook my hand and he must have thought I was struck dumb or something. And I guess I was. I couldn't speak, couldn't say a word, just stood there staring at him. My parents invited him to supper. And he said 'yes' just like that. I had no idea until he told me later that he felt it too. That we were meant to be together.

My parents killed a chicken, and added ham hocks, collards and corn bread, a lot better dinner then we usually had. But he knew we were poor. All I had was a hand-me-down dress from my sister that was already too small for me. He didn't care. I can still see how he looked at me. All I could see was him looking at me. I spilled my glass of milk that day right on the table just like a child. Probably had crumbs on my mouth as well as all over my dress. He didn't care. Just like that we knew we'd be together for the rest of our lives.

Mama and Daddy wouldn't hear about marriage. They made us wait a year hoping I'd give up the idea of marrying a preacher. We just waited them out. We knew what we wanted. And every Sunday I dragged my parents and sisters back to church. Didn't matter what the weather was. Didn't matter if I got a cold. Every Sunday I was in church. And I just sat in the pew ... and I worshipped him. I don't think God minded. If God is love, that was love.

The church was on fire one Sunday. People singin', clappin', dancin' hollerin', speakin' in tongues. You couldn't understand anything they were saying. All of a sudden I jumped up out of my chair and ran to the front of the church ... to the pulpit where Eddie stood and I touched his shining black robe ...it was on fire ... and I went screaming back to my chair.

And after the sermon, and the hymns, when things were quiet again he shook my hand and asked me about my schoolwork. But what he was really saying was 'I love you and we will be together soon.' I think Daddy finally heard him too and two days after my sixteenth birthday we got married in that very church. (beat) And I'm not leaving it now.

EVA

That is so romantic, Mrs. Pace.

MARY ALICE

(stands up) Who asked you little girl? You ... you ... get your hands off my grandson. Didn't I tell you a while ago you better not touch another thing in this house without asking?

EVA

(startled, she yanks her hand from JALANI's ; looks hurt; looks at Jalani; then slips her hand back into JALANI's. They hold hands tightly. EVA sits up straight)

Mrs. Pace I only meant to say that your story was so beautiful. I'm not trying to be rude to you and I really don't understand why you are treating me like I'm some slut or something. Because I'm White? For months leading up to this trip to Birmingham, Jalani talked on and on about how kind and loving you are, and I couldn't wait to meet you. (Pause) Now I wish I had never come here to this ... this ... place. (beat) But while I'm here I will respect your wishes and I won't touch any of your things without asking but with all due respect I don't need your permission to touch my own boy-friend.

(MARY ALICE sits back down in the armchair in silence and looks down at her lap. Everyone is awkwardly silent)

LORENZO

(Clearing his throat) Mama see what I mean? It is not like you at all to be rude to a guest in our house. That is proof that you don't need to be staying here by yourself all alone. This idea that you're not leaving? ... we'll just see about that.

MARY ALICE

We seen all about there is to see, Lorenzo, this is my home and this is where I stay. Now I'm ready for the will if y'all are done vexing me about my life. Jalani, will you look in the bottom shelf of your grandpa's desk and bring me the old brown box there?
(JALANI finds a cardboard box in the drawer and brings it to his grandmother. Everyone sits down. SHE opens the box and slowly removes various documents and objects.)

(takes out photo and hands it to LORENZO)

Here's our wedding picture. See how handsome your father was.

(LORENZO takes the photo. looks and passes it along to JALANI and EVA, and DAISY MAY).

FUNERAL DIRECTOR

(doorbell rings. JALANI goes to answer it and returns with FU-NERAL DIRECTOR who is the same man we will see as the SLAVE CATCHER and the SLAVE AUCTIONEER and the RAPIST in the historical scenes. MARY ALICE visibly recoils as HE enters as if SHE is afraid of HIM.)

Mrs. Pace, I've brought this paperwork from the Funeral Home. And you forgot these copies of Bishop Pace's birth certificate and social security card in our offices.

(He extends the paperwork but MARY ALICE keeps HER distance and does not extend HER hand to take the paperwork. It is an awkward moment. Finally LORENZO steps forward to take the papers.)

LORENZO

Thank you.

FUNERAL DIRECTOR

My condolences again. (receiving no response, HE turns to leave after another awkward moment.)

DAISY MAY

Let me show you out.

(THEY exit)

LORENZO

That was awkward.

MARY ALICE

That man gives me the creeps. I don't know why. I know that face, and it scares me.

LORENZO

He seems nice enough.

MARY ALICE

I don't know. It's like he's a ghost ... from one of my dreams.

(DAISY MAY returns, MARY ALICE pulls herself together)

LORENZO

Dream, Mama?

MARY ALICE

(paying no attention to LORENZO's words) Where were we?

LORENZO

The box.

MARY ALICE

Oh, yes. (returning to the box and withdrawing another paper) The will.

DAISY MAY

Maybe I better leave if y'all are doing family business.

MARY ALICE

Don't you worry, girl. There's no gold and no jewels so there's nothing to hide. You and your family know me as well as anyone in the world. (hands it to LORENZO) It's true, there really isn't any money saved up, I'm afraid. The house is free and clear though. You'll get everything when I go. The house deed. (hands to LORENZO) Our burial plot deeds ... (hands it to LORENZO) ... for us to be together right here in Birmingham. That's all there is.

JALANI

What's that Big Momma? (pointing into the box)

MARY ALICE

(SHE pauses. HE reaches into the box and draws out a smaller wooden box with a rusted and obviously old metal lock)

Just junk got in there somehow.

JALANI

Look at this. This is like ancient. I mean really, really ancient, all rusted and stuff.

74

(HE passes the locked box to EVA who passes it to LORENZO, and
DAISY MAY. EACH takes a minute examining it)

What is this Grandma?

LORENZO

Why is that in here, Mama?

MARY ALICE

I told you, some old junk your daddy threw in there, that's all.

LORENZO

In the box? ... Daddy threw this in that box with these important
papers? ... Dad kept files, he was very organized, he didn't throw
stuff in his desk. He didn't put anything in his desk that he didn't
think was extremely important.

DAISY MAY

The box, Lorenzo.

(HE looks at HER. SHE looks at HIM meaningfully, referring to
their earlier conversation)

The box.

LORENZO

(HE gets it) The box ... the box you and Daddy were fighting and
arguing about?

MARY ALICE

I told you, me and your daddy never fought about anything, not
anything.

LORENZO

(beat) Mama, are you hiding something from me? When you get
short like that I know there is something else behind it.

MARY ALICE

There's no such thing, Lorenzo, I don't know what you're talking about.

LORENZO

That's exactly what you always say. Whether you were trying to hide my birthday presents when I was a kid or trying to hide some bill we couldn't pay and I'd find it and you'd always say: (mimics HER) 'I don't know what you're talking about'. Don't try to fool me like you did when I was a kid. I'm on to you, Mama. What does this mean? Why did Papa keep this?

MARY ALICE

Just an old lock in an old box. A silly old lock. Doesn't mean anything.

LORENZO

Why was it in there, Mama? Come on, it has to mean something. What would dad have hung on to this old thing for in the first place?

MARY ALICE

I have no idea. I told you ... Now I don't feel too well. Give me that.

(LORENZO, hesitates and then hands over lock. MARY ALICE tosses it dismissively back into the desk)

Old junk, we'll just put this away. I'm tired I need to rest. You all wear me out. I'm going to go work on one of my quilts in the sewing room. Y'all excuse me. Daisy, you know your own way out. (SHE rises and exits. The others watch HER go)

JALANI

What was that all about, Pops?

LORENZO

Don't know, Son.

DAISY MAY

I'm sorry, Lorenzo, I didn't mean to make trouble. Maybe I was wrong about the box. Maybe there was another box.

LORENZO

No, I don't think so, Daisy. I do know Daddy didn't save junk in his desk for nothing. That was a desk for business and that man was extremely organized for business. Everything in its place and a purpose to everything. Maybe we can get her to tell us more about it tomorrow.

DAISY MAY

I best be headin' home, y'all

(ALL stand and DAISY MAY makes as to leave. LORENZO approaches HER to show HER out)

You know, Lorenzo, I know you're leavin' tomorrow and all but there's an ice cream social down at the church tonight—

LORENZO

I'd love to go, Daisy.

DAISY MAY

—and I was wondering ... (shocked) You would?

LORENZO

I think I would. You know for some reason I never really noticed before how kind you are ... and how pretty.

DAISY MAY

Oh, Lorenzo. (flustered) (beat) People always said they just thought of me and Maisy as two peas in a pod, as one person even, didn't notice me.

LORENZO

I don't think so. Maisy is a little—

(DAISY MAE puts HER finger to HIS lips to stop HIM from saying anything negative about MAISY)

You are kind ... and quite beautiful.

(SHE gives HIM a quick peck on the cheek and turns and practically runs out of the house.)

JALANI

Oh ... my ... God!

LORENZO

I may be old, Jalani, but I ain't dead yet. That is one fine looking woman.

JALANI

Ewwww, Dad—

EVA

I think she's terrific, Mr. Pace. And she obviously likes you.

LORENZO

Well, it's jut a church ice cream social is all, doesn't mean anyone's getting married or anything. Now, where were we—

JALANI

You know, Pops, I've been meaning to talk to you about something.

LORENZO

Yeah? What is it, boy?

JALANI

Maybe now's not a good time, if you're upset.

LORENZO

No go ahead. I'm o.k. Bring it on.

JALANI

Well, it's about me going to college—

LORENZO

About Morehouse?

EVA

Oh, suddenly I'm tired too. Well, I'll go paint my nails, or lie down or do my hair or something ... and see you both later. (SHE quickly exits)

LORENZO

This is getting stranger and stranger. What's up, Jalani? Come on, man, spit it out.

JALANI

Pops, I really, really, want to stay in New York and go to NYU. (rushing to defend HIMSELF before his father can argue). We can be together. We can save money while I live at home with you. NYU has a great Psych program, Murchison and Booker teach there and you know I want to do Depth Psychology like them and I've already got a few Concurrent Enrollment courses there ...

LORENZO

Slow down, slow down. And I suppose it is no coincidence to this sudden interest in NYU that Eva will be there also?

JALANI

Pop ... the academics are top notch at NYU, you know that. Top professors. The cost is low. I get to stay in New York And ... (beat), yeah, Eva will be there.

LORENZO

All the Pace men went to Morehouse, Bro. (ticking them off on his fingers) Your great grandfather. Your grandfather. Me. (Pointing last finger at JALANI) Now, you. We have to keep up the Pace tradition.

JALANI

Not me, Pops. Not me. (beat) Please.

LORENZO

I ain't payin' for any college but Morehouse, Son.

JALANI

You can't make me go.

LORENZO

(Becoming angry) You don't think so?

JALANI

(standing up for HIMSELF) No, I don't think so.

LORENZO

I could toss your ungrateful ass out of the house ... I could never speak to your sorry self again ... I could turn my back on you, Boy, and walk away .

JALANI

You can't be the boss of me forever. I've got to do this, Pops ... for me. I can't just do what you want for me to do anymore. I've got to make decisions for myself. And you got to let me make my own mistakes.

LORENZO

Mistakes is right. (LORENZO starts to raise HIS voice) What would your mama say?

80

JALANI

She'd say you can't be the Great Dictator all the time. Just like she said when she was alive.

LORENZO

(Balling up a fist and advancing on JALANI as if to strike HIM) Damnit, boy, you take that back. You ungrateful punk. I brought you into this world and I can take you out—

(LORENZO strikes JALANI. JALANI is momentarily shocked. Then HE strikes back. A fight ensues. LORENZO wrestles JALANI to the ground. JALANI struggles on the floor to escape. LORENZO rises and drags him back by HIS leg. JALANI kicks LORENZO off. LORENZO lands on HIS butt, HIS eyes wild with rage. JALANI stands)

JALANI

(He is on the verge of tears.) I'm a man. I'm a man too, just like you.

LORENZO

Man, my ass. You're just a dumb n- boy doesn't know shit from—

JALANI

(Shouting) I am a man! I could be ... I could be anything. I could be a psychiatrist someday like I want. You don't know. I could be ... (beat) I could be President some day.

LORENZO

(Jumps up and advances on JALANI) A nigga like you could never be President of 'The United States of White America.' Why do you think they call it the 'White House, dummy?' It ain't never gonna be the 'Black House!'

(LORENZO leaps upon JALANI, grabs him by the neck with one hand and is about to strike him in the face with HIS fist)

MARY ALICE

(Enters parlor) What in Lawd's sakes is going on in here?

LORENZO

(dropping HIS fist to HIS side, calming HIMSELF slowly and
straightening HIS clothes. JALANI does likewise)

Nothing, Mama, nothin' at all.

JALANI

Nothing, Big Mama.

MARY ALICE

Pretty loud 'nothing,' you two.

LORENZO

It's just that this ungrateful ... child—

JALANI

I ain't no child.

LORENZO

This. Ungrateful. Child. doesn't know what's good for him.

MARY ALICE

And you thought hitting him would make him 'grateful?'

LORENZO

(hanging HIS head, controlling HIMSELF, now ashamed) No,
Mama. (facing JALANI) I'm sorry, Son.

(JALANI runs out of the parlor. LORENZO watches HIM go)

Now I've blown it. God, I'm a lousy father.

MARY ALICE

You are no such thing, Lorenzo. You raised that boy through the toughest times on your own. He knows that ... and he knows you love him.

LORENZO

I hope so. (long pause)

MARY ALICE

Was it about Morehouse?

LORENZO

How did you—

MARY ALICE

Oh, he tried to get me to talk you outa' makin' him go there.

LORENZO

(angry all over again) That little ... ungrateful squirt.

MARY ALICE

You know he's a good boy, Lorenzo. Times change ... people been tellin' ME that anyway (gives LORENZO a meaningful look).

LORENZO

(still angry) Ahhhg! Strength, Lord, give me strength. (beat) I feel like I am fighting on two fronts at the same time and everyone is dug in for trench warfare. All right then, I'll drop the bomb. Mama, I didn't really want to tell you this but (long beat) I hated Morehouse.

MARY ALICE

You did? ... You never told us that? ... For God's sake, why?

LORENZO

I didn't want to hurt your feelings then, Mama. (beat) I don't really want to hurt your feelings now. Forget it.

MARY ALICE

No more forgettin' things, Lorenzo. You tell me the truth right now. Why didn't you like Morehouse.

LORENZO

Oh, Morehouse was fine, I guess. It was great, you know, for some people. Just not me. It was just that everyone there knew the Pace name. It was always 'Oh, you're Bishop Pace's son aren't you?' Nobody knew me, Lorenzo Pace, just Eddie Pace's son. Some of the old guys even remembered the name Joseph Pace, granddad. A name can be a burden sometimes. A burden or a blessing. Sometimes both.

MARY ALICE

It's an important name. The Pace name stands for something. You should have been proud of it.

LORENZO

That's the past, Mama, and I wanted my own name for my own time.

MARY ALICE

There's no escaping the past, Lorenzo. The past grabs you by the neck and drags you back. The past sticks thoughts and memories down your throat until you gag. I know the past, Lorenzo, the past strangles you till you can't breathe. (SHE seems to enter a reverie that is HERS alone).

LORENZO

What do you mean, Mama?

(SHE makes no answer but slowly leaves the stage.)

End Scene 4

84

Act 1

Scene 5

Video rolls on the screen, we see herds of wildebeest, the jungle, water holes, animal migrations.

We see a map of Africa and then the film zooms in to focus on West Africa, the area around Senegal and Mali, the so-called Slave Coast. Drums start playing softly and then increase in volume.

As the video fades actors costumed as animals (feathered as birds, carrying poles as tall giraffes, furred as lions, hyenas, etc.) enter from both sides.

African music, drums, dance.

AFENYI enters dressed as a member of the Dogon people. SHE is the same actor who portrays MARY ALICE. SHE is wearing a distinctive necklace that will be seen each time SHE appears. SHe stops to listen to a bird. SHE sets down HER basket The drums continue playing. SHE pauses to satisfy HIS thirst at a water hole.

The drumming fades as the music of a refined European Minuet rises (a J.S. Bach orchestral suite?). Men dressed as European soldiers enter stage left and spy AFENYI. THEY slowly approach HER, When AFENYI sees their approach SHE darts to HER right but a third soldier, the same actor who plays the FUNERAL DIRECTOR, steps forth and grabs HER. The other two soldiers move deliberately over and all lay hands on AFENYI. SHE screams and resists. THEIR actions are slow, methodical and deliberate, like an assembly line of bondage. THEY toss aside HER basket. The idea is that they have done this many times before and have it down to a choreographed routine in time to the stately, restrained music of the European minuet. At some point THEY tilt AFENYI horizontally and wrap HER body in chains with a care that reminds us of gently swaddling an infant. SHE is now totally helpless.

One SOLDIER reaches into his kit and removes the same lock we saw in the Pace parlor and holds it up high over HIS head. Then HE closes the lock over AFENYI'S chains, securing her. The three SOLDIERS bodily carry AFENYI off stage. The Minuet fades. The drumming returns with intensity and then softly fades. After a few moments the drumming abruptly ceases. Lights down on stage as ALL exit.

End Act 1

Act 2

Scene 1

AT RISE: EVA BARNES is again sitting in a chair wrapped in the
same quilt as before. She is alone reading.
MARY ALICE enters suddenly. Eva jumps up and the quilt falls to
the floor.

EVA

Ms. Pace, I ... I ... can explain about the quilt! I was chilly and it
was laying there so colorful and snuggly and I just couldn't resist
... I ...

MARY ALICE

(SHE picks up the quilt) Sit down Eva. I saw the light on and wondered who else besides me would be up so late.

(EVA looks puzzled She slips into the chair and watches MARY
ALICE pace the room, agitated.)

I've been having the same dream these past few nights. A
dream ... but it's so vivid, so real. I just don't know what it's about.
It won't let me rest. Like it wants something from me.

EVA

They say dreams are entries to our unconscious ... to unresolved
issues and problems ...

MARY ALICE

That Doctor Freud, huh? He was Jewish too, right?

EVA

So? Freud was more into sexual explanations for everything.
Dream analysis today considers more of a total gestalt for—

MARY ALICE

Total what?

EVA

Total gestalt. It's not just about sex—

MARY ALICE

I coulda' told you that.

EVA

—but about our whole lives. The things we can't work out in our waking lives, the things that worry us or make us uneasy, pop up in our dreams when our defenses are down. Sometimes dreams try to make us face our fears. Do you want to tell me about it?

MARY ALICE

(SHE sits) No. (long pause) It was about people who looked familiar. I don't know. In the jungle or something.

EVA

The jungle?

MARY ALICE

There were drums ... and soldiers.

EVA

Like a war?

MARY ALICE

No. Not a war. Like a kidnapping. (beat) Forget it. It's not important. (picking quilt up off floor and folding it up) Eva. (beat). I thought about all that happened yesterday. I admit that I do have a real problem with you.

EVA

How can you have a problem with me? You just met me.

MARY ALICE

Well first off I don't like this idea of interracial dating. Second. It seems Jalani was fine with attending Morehouse until you came along. Third. It seems like you completely disrespect our family name and all that it represents.

EVA

Well first off Ms. Pace the world has changed when it comes to Blacks and Whites dating. Jalani and I are in love whether you like it or not. Second. Jalani has his own mind and knows what he wants. And what he wants is to go to school in New York. And third. I don't see what the big deal is about a family name and all that it represents. My family name is a big lie and doesn't mean anything to me. It does not define who I am. I define who I am.

MARY ALICE

(Laughs bitterly) This is worse than I thought. On top of being a White girl, you're a smart White girl with a smart mouth. Child, didn't your parents raise you to respect your elders?

EVA

You get respect when you give respect Mrs. Pace.

MARY ALICE

(MARY ALICE bolts out of HER chair) Listen to me, Eva. (jabbing HER finger at EVA angrily). After all I've been through the past few weeks I'm just plain tired. I'm tired in my mind and I'm tired in my heart … (jabbing at EVA's chest with HER finger) … and I don't want to fight folks anymore about what's right and what's wrong and what's best for me and what's not. I've had my time with the only man I've ever loved and now he's gone. (drops HER finger from tiredness as much as the passing of HER anger. Big exhale of breath.) All those years and now it seems like it went by in a blink of an eye so you are absolutely right about one thing.

EVA

I am? I'm right ... about what?

MARY ALICE

You and Jalani. It doesn't matter what I think. Life is short, so live it to be happy—you and him. But know this young lady, you will never be fulfilled in your heart if you believe that you alone are the one who defines you.

EVA

What do you mean by that?

MARY ALICE

I mean you are defined by a lot more than just you.

EVA

I disagree, with all due respect, ma'am.

MARY ALICE

Tell me Eva. What do YOU mean when you say your name is a lie?

EVA

My great grandfather was Andrzej Barnovski, a Jewish peddler from Poland. He got off the ship at Ellis Island and some idiot immigration officer couldn't understand the name Barnovski . So he told my great grandfather his name was Barnes. My great grandfather never changed it back. So my name is a fraud. An invention to blend in, to be American. End of story. Just a way to forget about the Cossacks, the burning of the synagogues, the anti-Semitism, the rapes of Jewish women in the old country.

MARY ALICE

Rapes ... Did you say rapes?

EVA

Rape was like a weapon they used to terrify the Jews. To defile them, humiliate them.

MARY ALICE

I know, girl. I know how that works. Ain't nothing worse than rape. A lot of half Black babies come out of White men raping Black women. (long beat) Look Eva, sounds to me like there's nothing wrong with your name except you. You're ashamed of something that happened in the past.

EVA

I'm not ashamed. I just—

MARY ALICE

You just remind me of June Bensen. Trying to deny her roots.

EVA

Who? What are you talking about?

MARY ALICE

June Bensen, Maisy and Daisy's aunt. So light-skinned she could pass for White ... so she did. She spent her life living a lie. She never knew who she really was.

EVA

But it was my great-grandfather who went along with the name Barnes, not me!

MARY ALICE

So who exactly is to blame for the fact that you are happy to walk around sporting this hoity toity name with no regard for your real name and heritage or that of your Black boyfriend? You being a Jew, you of all people, should respect the fact that you come from an oppressed people. African Americans know exactly what it is like to fight oppression and to have a last name that's not our "real name." But we are proud of the names we have and we're proud of where we have come from. (Beat) (Chuckles). Well most of us are proud, except for June Bensen, bless her heart.

EVA

(Giggles) I guess I never thought of it that way and I'm sorry. I didn't realize how much the Pace name really means. I mean I know about slavery and all but I guess I didn't think about the fact that Jalani's ancestors and my ancestors do have some things in common. (beat) Mrs. Pace can we start over with getting to know each other?

MARY ALICE

(Stands) I don't know if it is possible to do such a thing as start over when you get to be my age. There's just so much to let go of. We'll see. (MARY ALICE starts to exit. Then SHE turns and hands the quilt back to EVA.) We can try.

(EVA watches until Mary Alice is gone. She slowly wraps HER-SELF up in the quilt and starts reading again)

End Scene 1

Act 2

Scene 2

SETTING: Later the same night. The same parlor as earlier. AT RISE: the parlor is dark. Some moonlight enters through a window. A shadowy figure enters. It is JALANI. He heads towards the desk but stubs his toe on an unseen table leg in the dark and audibly groans. HE rubs his toe as HE is barefoot. HE recovers and moves again towards the desk. Just as he reaches the desk and removes the box from the desk, EVA enters from a guest bedroom off the parlor, flips on a light switch against one wall and a ceiling light comes on. She holds an iron poker from the fireplace.

EVA

What are you up to?

JALANI

God, you scared me.

EVA

You scared me. I thought it was a burglar or something. (puts down poker) Or maybe my boyfriend heading for my room.

JALANI

Shush. They'll hear you. There's no fooling around in Big Momma's house.

EVA

(gesturing to box in HIS hands) What do you call that then?

JALANI

Not fooling around, researchin'. I just wanted a look.

(HE looks around all sides of the box. HE pulls the locked box out of the desk and holds it up high over his head to look at it. EVA moves to HIS side).

92

EVA

Look at that iron. It's so old. What do you think it was used for? Why did your grandpa save it?

JALANI

(He shakes his head) We may never know.

(The lights dim. EVA and JALANI freeze and go silent. In the dark THEY exit the stage.)

End Scene 2

ACT 2

Scene 3

Video projections of historical renderings of the Middle Passage, as slaves are packed into ships and brought across the Atlantic. (Gospel Choir sings "Sometimes I Feel Like a Motherless Child," "Swing Low Sweet Chariot," etc.) We see the crowded conditions, slaves tossed overboard, slaves disembarked in the U.S. south, and then photos of slaves on the auction block. AFENYI is led in by soldiers and placed on an auction block. SHE is dressed in rags and faces directly out at the audience. SHE wears chains and the lock that binds them together at HER waist is the same lock we have seen before. SHE wears the same unique necklace at HER neck. Bruises and the marks of the whip can be seen on HER body. SHE turns first to one side and then the other as if instructed to by the man selling HIM. SHE turns HER back to the audience which sees the mark of the lash on HER body. The AUCTIONEER is the same actor as the FUNERAL DIRECTOR/SOLDIER/SLAVER.

AUCTIONEER

Going once!

(The video projection switches to historical photos of slaves working in the fields, whipped slaves displaying their wounds and maimings, arms or legs amputated, for trying to escape, interspersed with historical wanted posters for escaped slaves, photos of Harriet Tubman, Frederick Douglass, Abraham Lincoln, and photos and illustrations of the Civil War.)

Going twice!
Going three times! Sold! to Mr. Thomas Hardaway. One teenage n- girl for $695!

(Stage darkens slowly until there is a single spotlight on AFENYI. Then it goes off and there is Darkness.)

End Scene 3

Act 2

Scene 4

SETTING: Back in the Pace Parlor as in Act 1, Scene 1 but the following day. AT RISE: the parlor is empty of people. Then MARY ALICE enters pursued by LORENZO.

LORENZO

That's all there is to it, Mama, you have to come.

MARY ALICE

Don't you dare tell me what is and what is not, what I can and cannot do. Or, what I have to do! Huh!

LORENZO

Sorry, Mama. We are just looking out for you, trying to do what's best for you, sweet Mama. (HE gestures for HER to sit). Please, Mama. I ... Jalani and I ... want you to come up to New York and live with us. We need you. Since my beautiful Berniece died we're lonely. I'm a terrible cook. I can't keep the house clean all by myself. Jalani lacks a real mother and I spend way too many hours on campus, not just teaching but in committee meetings, meetings with students ... Jalani needs someone to be there when he gets out of school. Someone to keep an eye on him. He's at an age when he could be getting into trouble, Hanging out with a rough crowd ... Jalani needs you. Come stay with us. Please, Mama, please.

(Puts his hands together as if beseeching HER)

MARY ALICE

You don't fool me, Lorenzo. You and Jalani have done just fine for these years since Berniece passed. Jalani is a fine young man and you have no reason to worry about him. Just like you have no reason to worry about me.

LORENZO

Let's face facts, Mama. You're 75 year old—

MARY ALICE

Not for two more months—

LORENZO

—and you need some help. What if you—

MARY ALICE

I've never fallen in my life.

LORENZO

Jalani had to help you get up off the floor just two days ago.

MARY ALICE

I didn't fall ... I slipped ... on a rug that got tangled up in my feet.
Just the kind of accident that could have happened to anybody,
even you.

LORENZO

It didn't happen to anybody. It happened to you. Alone in this big
empty house by yourself. What if a burglar comes in here ... (looks
around, points to window) ... right through that window in the
night. You are totally defenseless. What if someone came in here
with a gun ... or ... the house catches on fire? Me way up there in
New York and you down here by yourself. I wouldn't feel com-
fortable leaving you alone, Mama, I just want you to be safe. Just
because I love you and worry all the time.

MARY ALICE

I know you do, Son. And I love you more than anything in this
world. I want you to be safe too. (beat) After you were born Eddie
and I tried to have more children. Two miscarriages—

LORENZO

Two? Mama, you had two miscarriages? I never knew that.

MARY ALICE

Two, a boy and a girl. You were still too young to know. The first
time I just started bleeding and when I got to the hospital they just
couldn't save her. One I lost right here in this house one night ...
We just told you Mama was visiting her sister for a few days.
You were all we had and you were enough, more than enough.
You made us so proud. Graduating from Morehouse with honors,
getting the position teaching art at City College. Eddie bragged
on you to all his friends. He loved you very much. But my life is
almost over, Lorenzo, let me finish it here in my house, with all my
friends, my church, my memories.

LORENZO

(submissively, but not yet resigned) Mama. (Hugs HER and kisses
HER on the cheek)

MARY ALICE

(SHE is having none of it) Don't 'mama' me, Lorenzo, I've seen too
much sorrow and trouble in my life to have you be the boss of me
now. No more, you hear! My boss just died!

(SHE exits to the kitchen, leaving Lorenzo stunned by HER out-
burst. The doorbell rings. Sound of door opening and closing)

(offstage) Well, girlfriend, we are certainly seeing more of you than
usual lately. I hope you ain't brought another pie—

DAISY MAY

No, ma'am—

MARY ALICE

Because you bring one more pie in this house and we all gonna get
fat.

DAISY MAY

No, no pie this time, Miz Pace.

MARY ALICE

Well o.k. then, What'd you want? And where's that pretty sister of yours?

DAISY MAY

Oh, Maisy's workin' on a project. I just thought I'd see Lorenzo and how he's—

MARY ALICE

Ah, ha, ah, ha. Well, come on in then, come on in, child.

DAISY MAY

Thank you.

(MARY ALICE and DAISY MAY enter the parlor where LORENZO rises from a chair)

MARY ALICE

Well, Son, look what the cat dragged in.

LORENZO

Great to see you again, Daisy.

DAISY MAY

And you, Lorenzo.

MARY ALICE

Well, I guess I'll go back to the kitchen and work on lunch. (beat) unless you still need protection, Lorenzo.

LORENZO

(very quickly) No, Mama ... you go on. I'll be just fine.
(MARY ALICE exits after a final look at EACH)DAISY MAY

I just wanted to say—

LORENZO

(Simultaneously)
—I had a great time last night.

DAISY MAY

(Simultaneously)
—I had a great time last night.

(THEY both laugh)

DAISY

I know you're going back up North soon.

LORENZO

Maybe tomorrow. Soon. I don't really know. Everything is kinda'
in an uproar here. Nothing is going like I planned. But then, it
never does!

DAISY MAY

No, things often don't. I thought when Daddy died our lives would
change dramatically. But they didn't. Maisy's still making bookcases just like when Papa was alive.

LORENZO

Still with the bookcases?

DAISY MAY

She's over there makin' one now. I swear, if I spend one more
day listening to that crazy woman hammer and saw I am going
to scream. There are only so many damn bookcases one can use,
Lorenzo, even for an educated man like you.

LORENZO

I'm sure that's true, Daisy.

DAISY MAY

What's wrong, Lorenzo.

LORENZO

(HE gestures for HER to sit and HE does also)

I can't get anyone to do what they should.

DAISY MAY

What they should do ... or what you want them to do?

(HE shoots HER a look)

I'm sorry if I spoke out of turn.

LORENZO

No ... you're probably right. It is what I want and I thought it was
what they needed. Now I don't know. I wanted Mama to come
North with us and I wanted Jalani to go to Morehouse. There's
nothing wrong with that, is there?

DAISY MAY

No, of course not. But—

LORENZO

But?

DAISY MAY

I found out, first with Poppa, and now with Maisy, that however
right you are, people are still stubbornly going to do what they
think is right for their own selves. And the harder we push the
more committed they are to their own way. People are free, Lorenzo and freedom can be terrifying sometimes.

LORENZO

Tell me about it. Whatever happened to we give the orders and they do as they're told. Maybe slavery wasn't all bad.

DAISY MAY

I think it's better this way, Lorenzo.

LORENZO

I know. (beat) I had a great time goin' to the ice cream social with you last night, Daisy.

DAISY MAY

Me too, Lorenzo.

LORENZO

You ever been to New York, Daisy?

DAISY MAY

No. It seems so big.

LORENZO

Bigger than all the people in the state of Alabama. But, I've got a nice place there. And I could show you around—

DAISY MAY

Yes.

LORENZO

—and I think ... Yes?

DAISY MAY

Yes, I'd love to visit you in New York.

LORENZO

I think that would be ... great.

(With trepidation and some awkward maneuvering THEY shyly
kiss)

DAISY MAY

(flustered) I better go ... Maisy'll be looking for me.

(SHE exits hurriedly)

LORENZO

(LORENZO looks into space at DAISY's exit. MARY ALICE enters
quietly. LORENZO starts when he sees HER.)

I didn't hear you, Mama. What you doin'?

MARY ALICE

It's my house, Lorenzo ... What do you mean what am I doing? I
am walking in my house. (beat) but I did you hear you with Daisy
May ... and I think you got the wrong sister.

LORENZO

What?

MARY ALICE

Maisy Day is the girl for you.

LORENZO

I don't think so, Mama, lessen' I need some new bookshelves.

MARY ALICE

You know what they say: 'If you're black, stay back; if you're
brown, stick around; if you're yellow, you're mellow; ... and if
you're white, you're all right.' Daisy ain't White but she looks too
pale to me.

LORENZO

Ain't no color to kindness, Mama, and it's been a long time since I've seen kindness in a woman.

(HE exits. MARY ALICE stands alone, perplexed)

End Scene 4

Act 2

Scene 5

The stage is dark. There is the sound of night insects. We see a gobo of the moon covered in clouds. AFENYI enters Stage Right quietly and stealthily. SHE appears frightened.

SLAVE MASTER

(offstage) I know you're there. (stumbles over a dead branch) God Damn it! (Gets up) I'll find you.

(THOMAS HARDAWAY, AFENYI's master enters. AFENYI tries to evade HIM in the dark but HE finally grabs HER. SHE fights back. THEY struggle. HE paws at HER body. This is an assault. Finally he draws back and hits her brutally with HIS fist. SHE is hurt. HE throws her over HIS shoulder and THEY exit the stage. (beat) We hear HER scream from off stage. SHE staggers back onto the stage pursued by THOMAS HARDAWAY who has a large knife. As HE is about to strike AFENYI, MARY ALICE HARDAWAY appears carrying a lantern attracted by AFENYI's screams. THOMAS sees HER, drops the knife and runs off stage. MARY ALICE moves slowly to AFENYI. SHE sees HER beaten on the ground. SHE puts down HER lantern and very slowly begins to comfort AFENYI. The sounds of the night insects return.)

End Scene 4

Act 2

Scene 6

SETTING: The Pace Parlor later that same day.
AT RISE: JALANI is holding the old box again. He takes out the lock and tosses it to EVA.

JALANI

Catch.

EVA

(catching the lock) Hey, be careful with that. It's old and you don't want to break it. (looks at lock and pulls at the hasp) I wonder if we could get it open?

JALANI

(gets up and moves to EVA) Give it here. Let me try.

(SHE gives him lock. He pulls on it mightily to no avail.)

Damn. That's rusted solid.

(LORENZO enters parlor)

Hey, Dad, can you open it?

(flips lock to LORENZO. LORENZO turns lock over in his hand, gives the hasp a tug. Sits down. Begins pulling harder on the lock as MARY ALICE enters)

MARY ALICE

You'll never get that old thing open again. Eddie never could ... (SHE realizes SHE has said too much)

LORENZO

What did you say? (beat) He couldn't, huh? So it's not in here by mistake. I knew Dad saved it for a reason. Come on, Mama, level with me. You been trying to hide something from me? (He slams the box down on the coffee table)

MARY ALICE

(trying to cover HER slip) I didn't say anything.

LORENZO

You said Dad tried to open this lock.

MARY ALICE

Did I? ... Well, maybe he did. So what?

LORENZO

So, it means something. There was a reason he tried to open it. There was a reason he saved it. And you know what it is.

MARY ALICE

Leave it alone, Lorenzo. Stop trying to interrogate me like I'm some criminal.

LORENZO

Tell me, Mama ... Please.

MARY ALICE

(shouting) I said leave it alone. (SHE begins to cry)

LORENZO

Mama. Please don't cry. You know I can't stand to see you cry. (HE tries to comfort HER) Is it that painful? Wait a minute. (HE gets up and retrieves the old box and lock. Holds it) This is the box, isn't it, Mama, just like I thought. Daisy May was right, wasn't she? This is that box, isn't it Mama? The box the Bensen sisters heard you and Papa yelling about years ago.

MARY ALICE

Oh, God, Lorenzo, oh, God. (beat) That was 20 years ago and those gals remember that.

(SHE cries. ALL surround HER and comfort HER)

Yes, Lorenzo. I ... I wasn't ... truthful. I am so sorry.

LORENZO

For what, Mama? (beat) It's o.k. It's o.k. Every couple fights. It's just an old box and an old lock.

(HE looks at JALANI and EVA, not knowing what to do)

Forget it, Mama, just forget it. We'll throw this piece of scrap away and forget it. Don't cry, Mama, don't cry. Nothing is worth seeing you like this. Forgive me for pressing the issue. Just forget about it. We'll pretend we never saw it. I promise. I won't mention it again.

MARY ALICE

(regaining control) I am sorry for ... all the ... untruths, Lorenzo, for so many untruths. Maybe it's time for that to end. I was so ashamed, so ashamed. (takes the lock in HER hands) I told Eddie again and again to throw this out. But he never would. He sat right there at that desk holding it, trying to open it. We argued and fought. That one day it got so awful, the Bensens must have heard me yelling.

LORENZO

Why, Mama? Why wouldn't dad throw this away?

MARY ALICE

(Beat) It was all he had of his grandmother.

LORENZO

His grandmother? All right. Let me get this. His father, my grandfather was Joseph Pace, right?

MARY ALICE

Joseph Allen Pace.

107

LORENZO

And he was born just after the Civil War, right?

MARY ALICE

Yes, in 1866, right here in Birmingham.

LORENZO

And Dad said he ran a store, a dry goods shop?

JALANI

Yeah, I never got that, Pops, what are 'dry goods?'

EVA

You know, men's and women's clothes, cloth for sewing, sundries and notions.

(THEY look at HER perplexed.

LORENZO

Sundries? ... Whatever? And he was married to Alice Pace. So who was Dad's grandfather, the father of Joseph Allen Pace? My great grandfather? Who was my great grandmother?

JALANI

My great, great grandfather and great, great grandmother.

MARY ALICE

My grandfather was Ezekiel. Ezekiel's wife was named Alice.

JALANI

(together) Ezekiel and Alice Pace?

MARY ALICE

Just Ezekiel ... and just plain Alice. Alice wasn't her real name.
We don't know her real name. They just called her ... Alice. Lord
knows where they got the name Pace. Just made it up most likely.

LORENZO

So just Alice?

MARY ALICE

They called her Alice. That's all the name she had. They said she
was his wife but they never had no wedding. They were from Africa.

JALANI

Africa?

MARY ALICE

From West Africa. The Gold Coast. We think. We can't know for
sure. Neither ever knew the name of their own country. I guess
there was no countries then. She said she was from the Dogon people. The Dogon live in the mountains.

LORENZO

An African named Alice? Exekiel? That doesn't make sense.

JALANI

Not Lumumba? or Mugabe? ... Alice and Ezekiel? What kind of
African names are those? Dad, you named me Jalani, that's African right?

MARY ALICE

We don't know their real names, Jalani. She only had but that one
name, Alice, her slave name.

JALANI

Slave name? My great, great grandmother was a slave? Wait a minute.

EVA

Don't you see, that explains some of these books I've been reading. Your grandfather was collecting these manuscripts, studying the family roots.

LORENZO

A slave? I mean Africa is cool. That's roots. The Great Zimbabwe. That's cool. Timbuktu—

EVA

The Great ... what?

LORENZO

The Great Zimbabwe—a Royal Palace built in 1,000 BC, in southern Africa, bigger than Paris. The Pyramids ... and on and on. We have a great history that no one wants to talk about. We were made ashamed of our history and ashamed to be from Africa. They made everybody believe we all lived in huts and ran around in animal skins.

EVA

Nefertiti! And Cleopatra—queen of Africa.

LORENZO

Well, they're not sure if the Egyptians were White or Black. There've been different theories. But think of it—Carthage which made even Rome tremble in fear, Timbuktu, Ethiopia's Queen of Sheba. Africa, the very continent where Adam and Eve arose in the Garden of Eden, the place where human life began. Africa, Mother of us all!

Give me a break, Lorenzo. Not great Africa. Not the Garden of
Eden. Just a place to catch slaves. Alice was a slave, Lorenzo, you
understand? Your great-grandmother was no more than a piece of
chattel, roped and bound, transported here as property, bred for
toil, branded like livestock, never legally married, never educated, an illiterate field hand. (Takes the lock) That history degrades
us all. You don't want to be known as no better than an animal?
Is that what you want for your son? (shakes hand with box at
JALANI) And Jalani, is that the family you want? Descended of a
woman hunted down, torn from her country, wrenched from her
family, penned on a ship like sheep, chained like beasts, without a
name? Is that what you want?

(HE shrinks back from HER rage)

(To EVA, with the lock still in HER fist) And you want that, girl?
Your people shackled her. Your people branded her. Your people
worked her without pay. Your people got rich off her sweat ... and
her blood.

EVA

Not me, Mrs. Pace—not my people—I'm Jewish. My people were
slaves in Egypt, remember? That's in Africa too. My family didn't
even come to this country until after slavery was abolished.

MARY ALICE

No, your people—your people, it doesn't matter if you're
Jew or Christian, if you were right here in slavery times or across
the sea, it's your people, White people, who did this, White people
who humiliated us, White people who raped us (SHE seems about
to cry) and now you come around and think my grandson will just
forget it all, forgive it all, and make cute little chocolate babies
with you?

(EVA shrinks back from these accusations)

Don't tell me you ... (SHE looks around at all three faces
one by one) ... and you, and you don't understand. Maybe it's different today. I don't know. But some things don't change. People
don't want animals in their homes and they don't want slaves in

their family trees. That's why I told Eddie all those years ago when his father gave him this box to throw it away and forget it. But he wouldn't do that. He just couldn't do it. Your grandfather was a great preacher. He earned a degree at Morehouse. Then he ran his own store. Your father was a great preacher. He earned a B.A. at Morehouse and a Master of Divinity at Emory. He served his church and his people honorably for thirty years.

Ezekiel ... Alice ... what absurd names, their owner's joke or nothing more than a bit of whimsy from a picture book, they could have named them Sambo or Aunt Jemima if they wanted to. But they chose the name of some Old Testament prophet just so they could laugh at him. 'Ezekiel' takes us down. They gave her the name of the plainest white trash, 'Alice.' Makes white people think of us not as college graduates, not as preachers, not as successful businesspeople, not as people at all, but as slaves, slaves they could order around, slaves they could breed, and whip, and buy and sell, and always, always, always feel superior to.

See this lock? It locks us up tight into the past. Locks us up as slaves and locks us out of America. Locks us into Aunt Jemima, and Sambo, and Step 'n Fetchit ... Kunta Kinte and Amos and Andy and every racist stereotype of every racist White man in America. (SHE cries again)

LORENZO

Mama, let it go, if it hurts that much.

MARY ALICE

I can't let it go. I can't ever let it go. You think Alice was the only slave? The only one they laughed at? You think she was the only one they beat? They beat me, Lorenzo. You think she was the only one they raped? They raped me, Lorenzo. They raped me! (Screaming) They raped ME! They raped ME!

LORENZO

(flinching away from HER as if slapped) What? What, Mama? Oh, no. I never knew. (HE steps back. Then forward and wraps HER in one of HER colorful quilts.)

MARY ALICE

They raped ME ... because they could. Because I was Black and female and and 15 years old and a granddaughter of slaves and they could do anything they wanted to me just like they did to her. Chained and locked (box still in HER hands). I was nothing just like she was nothing.

And I was pregnant. Eddie knew and he couldn't do anything ... somehow he stood by me.

(ALL surround HER and try to embrace HER in silence)

Lorenzo, I told you about those two babies I lost ... well, that first baby was born dead ... a White baby. We buried it ... under the house ... and forgot it ... but it never went away ... the shame never went away.

After we married, Eddie showed me this box his father gave him just before he died. This lock was put on Alice by the slavers (holds lock up). She was chained like a dog. Some time, after the Civil War, after Emancipation, Ezekiel and Alice gave this lock to their son, Joseph. Joseph gave it to Eddie. He meant to give it to you, and for you to give it to Jalani.

LORENZO

And you were going to lie to me, Mama, and throw it away? As if it meant nothing to Papa?

MARY ALICE

Don't you see, that's what we should do, shame should be thrown away. Buried and forgotten—like that White baby. We look forward not backward. We are Americans, not Africans. We are free, not slaves—

LORENZO

(shouting) But, Mama, we should be proud of our history and where we came from. I know it's painful. But we have this lock in our family that goes back to slavery. Think of it. This is history. Oh, stop it, Mama! (beat) You are so brave ... and I am so proud of you. Things happened to you that I can barely imagine and might never have survived. I am so proud of you.

MARY ALICE

I heard Eddie say those words so many years ago. I never knew if I could believe them.

LORENZO

He meant them, Mama, he truly did, just as I do. What happened to you ...what happened to Alice ... can't be forgotten or hidden or erased and it shouldn't be. It made us who we are today. Heads bowed, bones broken but our spirit is strong. Our spirit survived.

And Ezekiel and Alice, whoever they were, once had African names, like my son, like Jalani, a name of his people. And they were kidnapped and sold into slavery. Torn away from their parents. And maybe he was whipped and maybe she had to smile and say "yes massa" and "no massa" to save her life but they each survived.

And everyday as a slave they remembered their free life in Africa ... they remembered their family, a family just like us, and everyday as a slave they got up and worked in the fields in a dirty shirt and filthy pants or maybe waited table in the plantation house in a set of fine livery and did just what they were told, but they were never slaves in their hearts. Their hearts were free. That's why they survived. That's why they sucked up all that hate, all that fear, and survived. They lived. And their son lived and went to college, and their grandson lived and went to college and divinity school and their great grandson lived and went to college and teaches college today and Jalani is here and ready to begin his life only ... only because Ezekiel and Alice overcame, because they were never slaves in their souls. And Mama I am proud to be the great grandson of slaves—a great descendent of Ezekiel and Alice. (HE holds up the lock.) And I am proud to be your son. This lock is just a piece of metal, this box is just old wood. (He drops it.) It can't bring us down unless we let it.

(HE embraces HIS mother)

JALANI

(Bending down and picking up lock) Look. (Lifts it up to show others) It's open.

(The lock has opened.)

EVA

It ... popped open.

LORENZO

Must've been the fall on the floor.

JALANI

I don't know, Dad, that don't seem right. I couldn't pull it open.

LORENZO

Neither could I, Son.

MARY ALICE

Let me see that. (takes lock) I don't believe it. This hasn't been open in ... 100, ... no 150 years. Since Alice took it off when she got free.

EVA

Maybe this was the time.

JALANI

Look, there's a letter inside the box. (HE holds up an old piece of parchment with quill pen writing on it)

EVA

What does it say?

LORENZO

Hang on. Hang on. Mama.

(HE hands the letter to MARY ALICE who looks lost.)

MARY ALICE

This writing is awful small.

(looks around and spies MARY ALICE's glasses) Here.

MARY ALICE

(grudgingly) Thank you. (clears her throat) I, Afenyi Mu-
lumba, a free Black woman of 43 years of age, a member of the ...
Dogon ... nation and for 30 years a slave in the home of Thomas
Hardaway in the state of Alabama in the United States of America
do make this testimony before witnesses on this 27th day of June
1868.

Though I cannot write by my own hand, I do speak these
words as my own words to be written down in proper English by
the Union officer sitting before me today.

I was brought to the Hardaway plantation in 1838 after
being kidnapped from my home and held for months in a dirty
pen first on land and then on ship until I was placed for auction
in the city of Richmond, Virginia and bought for the plantation of
Thomas Hardaway and transported with 12 other Africans, none
of my own people, by wagon to the Hardaway plantation outside
Birmingham, in the state of Alabama.

I was put to work at first in the cotton fields and later in the
big house where I served as servant to Mary Alice Hardaway, wife
of Thomas, when I was called Alice after her.

EVA

Alice.

MARY ALICE

After Mary Alice. (reading the testimony again) It was
in their fields that I was attacked and ... raped ... (MARY ALICE
chokes up) ... Oh, my God ... attacked and raped by her husband,
my master, Thomas Hardaway. I will not dwell upon the details
except to say that he treated me like an animal.

Through these many years I was treated no better than a
beast of burden to be used as they wished by the White people who
owned me. I have never been able to return to my native land or
to see my parents and or little sisters, Thandeka and Morifa again.
They were very young when I was taken and I do not know if they
are living or dead, if they are with our people or if they too were
carried over the ocean into slavery.

I have lived these last years as husband and wife with Eze-kiel, known among his people, the Ogoni, as Jalani—

JALANI   LORENZO   EVA

(together) Jalani!

MARY ALICE

(long beat then reading again) ... and now we have a son. Though White people stole me from my family and White people worked me as an animal and a White man raped me I have learned not to hate all White people. A White woman saved my life. After raping me Thomas Hardaway meant to kill me. Mary Alice Hardaway stopped him even as he raised a knife to my throat and later nursed me back to health.
I am thankful that I had some learning since the end of the great war of and that today I can give my testimony so everyone will know the terrible misery we have lived with for years and that we people of Africa, the slaves, may never be forgotten. (MARY AL-ICE has come to the end of the letter)

LORENZO

This was in the box too.

(HE holds out AFENYI's necklace. HE hands it to MARY ALICE who examines it and then begins trying to put it on. EVA steps forward and helps MARY ALICE put on the necklace.)

MARY ALICE

Thank you, Eva.

(THEY embrace)

MARY ALICE

Maybe Alice was ready ... to be free. Free of the pain. Free of the shame. Free of all her suffering and beating of the 'yes, mass'a and 'no, sir.' Maybe we are ready ... I was wrong. I was wrong for so many years, Lorenzo. The lock is open—and we move into the future. I was locked but maybe I'm ready to be free. I know the past is the past—we can't escape that—but now we can enter and claim the future. The slaves always knew the day would come they would be free. Now I know this day I am free. (SHE looks at LORENZO) Alice would be proud of you, Lorenzo. She might think all that pain was worth it to see what her family became. (SHE looks at JALANI) And you are the future, Jalani. (Gives JALANI the lock) Alice gave our family this lock. We pass it down to each new generation to tell our story. Out of slavery we build freedom—out of shame we will build pride.

End Scene 6

Act 2

Scene 7

Later that same night. Suddenly a loud explosion. Sounds of broken glass, people running, screams Fire engine sirens. It is all reminiscent of the play's beginning. MAISY DAY and DAISY MAY enter Stage Left. THEY are dressed as if awakened from sleep, wearing pajamas, house coats, hair curlers.

MAISY DAY

Oh my Lord, the Pace house is on fire!

DAISY MAY

Lorenzo! Oh, my God, Lorenzo—I'm going in—

MAISY DAY

(grabs HER sister) No, it's too dangerous!

DAISY MAY

(struggling) Let me go!

MAISY DAY

(not letting go) Wait—look ... it's ... LORENZO

(LORENZO rushes in from stage Right)

LORENZO

Did they get out?

DAISY MAY

(DAISY MAY and LORENZO embrace)

We haven't seen anyone but you, Lorenzo.

LORENZO

I saw the smoke and flame ... I couldn't see anyone else ... I thought they had already gotten out ... I gotta go back in'

(sounds of fire engines draw nearer)

DAISY MAY

(grabs LORENZO) I'll go too.

MAISY DAY

Look!

(EVA staggers in from Stage Right. SHE are covered in soot and blackened. SHE is coughing.. More explosions and flames are heard behind HER)

LORENZO

(embraces HER) Thank God!—

EVA

She went back for the picture! (Coughing. Gasping for breath) Big Mama went back for her wedding picture!

LORENZO

Good Lord! Mama! Jalani! Stay right here.

DAISY MAY

(seeing Lorenzo is about to go into fire) No!

LORENZO

I have to. Wait right here. (long beat as they embrace) I love you

(He breaks the embrace and rushes into fire offstage. We see the flashing lights of emergency vehicles projected on the walls. Smoke fills the stage. A suspenseful time passes)

(LORENZO emerges from Stage Right looking even more black-ened and singed than anyone. HE is dragging JALANI. EVERY-ONE immediately embraces and hugs THEM)

Oh, my God!

(general shouting "Thank God!" "Praise the Lord!" "You're safe!" LORENZO embraces JALANI, and then DAISY MAY. MAISY DAY embraces JALANI. EVA embraces JALANI.)

MAISY DAY

Oh, my God. (beat) Mary Alice?!

(EVA and Daisy May look toward the offstage fire)

LORENZO

I was ... too late. She went back ... the fire ... the heat ... I couldn't reach her. (gasping for breath) I barely got Jalani.

(JALANI uncovers what is in HIS hands. It is the lock. HE shows to ALL and gives to LORENZO)

JALANI

(coughing) I got it. I had to get it.

LORENZO

(Embracing JALANI) Son ... my son ... you are the future. Mama chose to stay ... here ... (gives lock back to JALANI) You keep this . ... Mama knew—you are the future.

Gospel Choir sings "We shall be changed" and then: "The Negro National Anthem"

End Play

About the Authors

DR. LORENZO PACE is an artist, author, master story-teller and performance artist, and lecturer. Pace held his first exhibition at the School of the Art Institute in Chicago, where he graduated with both a BFA and an MFA. Pace went on to receive a doctorate in art education from Illinois State University and later made his home in New York City.

Pace works with a broad range of objects and materials. His sculptures, installations and performance art have received international acclaim and he has exhibited in galleries and museums all over the world, including New York City galleries, the National Civil Rights Institute in Birmingham, AL, as well as galleries in China, Brazil, Senegal, Suriname, Peru, and France. Pace has been featured in a variety of media, including the New York Times and New York Arts Magazine.

In 1993, Pace and his artwork rose to national attention when he was commissioned to build a monument at New York City's Foley Square paying homage to the African slaves originally buried on that site. In 1991, the remains of more than 400 African slaves were excavated during the construction of a federal building in the city's financial district. The City of New York wanted to create a memorial and Pace was chosen. His work resulted in a beautiful 300-ton granite sculpture named "Triumph of the Human Spirit." A replica of the lock that shackled Pace's great grandfather, Steve Pace, is a part of the base of the monument.

Pace is also author of four children's books, including *Jalani and the Lock,* which was described by Publisher's Weekly as a "stunning debut" and chosen as a "Best Book" by the *Los Angeles Times*. Other books by Pace are *Marching with Martin, Harriet Tubman and My Grandmother's Quilts*, and *Frederick Douglass and the North Star,* published this year.

Pace has served as Director of the Montclair State University (New Jersey) Art Gallery, a retired Professor of Art at the University of Texas—Rio Grande, and maintains a studio in Brooklyn, New York.

PHILLIP ZWERLING recently retired as an Associate Professor of Creative Writing and Director of the MFA Program in Creative Writing at the University of Texas Rio Grande Valley where he taught playwriting for ten years. He earned his M.Div. in Theology from Harvard University, his M.F.A. in Creative Writing from the University of New Orleans, and his Ph.D. in Theatre from the University of California, Santa Barbara. His plays have been produced on five college campuses and at Seaside Community Theater.

Scenes from his plays are anthologized in *One on One: The Best Women's Monologues for the Twentieth First Century*, *One on One: The Best Men's Monologues for the Twenty-First Century*, and *Duo:The Best Scenes for the Twenty First Century*, all by Applause Books. His play, "The History of Mexico: A Dream Play" appeared in the *Langdon Review*.

He is the author of three books: *Nicaragua: A New Kind of Revolution* (1985), *After School Theatre Programs for At Risk Teenagers*, (2007) and *Lee Blessing: A Critical Study of 44 Plays* (2015), the editor of one, *The CIA on Campus: Academic Freedom and the National Security State*, (2012) and co-author of another, *Eyes on Havana: The Memoir of An American Spy Betrayed by the CIA* (2018).

He lives in Fort Bragg, CA.

A black and white photograph of the lock that bound the chains of Lorenzo's great grandfather a slave. This lock is located in the African American History Museum in Washington D.C.

This play was inspired by the book *Jalani and the Lock*, written by Lorenzo Pace and published in 2000 by Rosen Publishing Group

The Triumph of the Human Spirit *sculpture by Lorenzo Pace sits at Black Lives Matter Blvd in New York City. The scuplture commemorates an African Burial Ground that was discoverd in 1991. Soaring high above Foley square, the sculpture symbolizes freedom and endurance. Besides its universal message, it was created with the artist's own personal ancestry in mind, and its granite Base contains a replica of the inherited lock and key which were used to enslave his great grandfather Steve Pace. Photograph by Elena Prokofyeva*

CPSIA information can be obtained
at www.ICGtesting.com
Printed in the USA
BVHW030913140521
607267BV00006B/758

9 781942 956860